EXPLORING THE WORLD BEYOND

A Real Astral Adventure

FranCelia Woodward

Library of Congress Catalog 99-73191
ISBN 1-58151-053-5

Cover Design by Richard Ferguson
Text Design by Kathie Clark-Lauer

BookPartners, Inc.
P.O. Box 922
Wilsonville, Oregon 97070

Dedication

This book is dedicated to those of you
who possess the spirit of adventure.
When you return from your astral explorations,
may you discover that Heaven is not in the World Beyond
but that it truly resides in your heart.

Love,

Fran Celia

Table of Contents

Preface

This book is the result of a change in my life that literally took place overnight when I experienced a *soul exchange*. Some refer to this as "becoming a walk-in." Before we incarnate, we choose not only our birth date but also our death date. Sometimes, at death, we leave behind a physical body that is in fairly good condition. Just as many people are now willing to donate parts of their body at death to help give life and health to others, there are some who agree to allow the physical body to be used by an incarnating Soul.

The Higher Self (Guardian Angel) of the person who is leaving his or her physical body through death and the Higher Self of the person who wishes to incarnate into an adult body must both approve of the plan. These two people need to be similar in vibration, just as in an organ transplant where there must be compatibility between the donor and the recipient.

Fran was thirty-six years old and several months pregnant when she and her husband, Don, and their two older sons drove to Seattle on vacation. Their younger son and daughter were staying with their grandma in California. On the fourth day of their vacation, the family decided to go up in Seattle's Space Needle. Fran had been complaining of severe pain, and when she became faint, Don realized that he needed to take her to a hospital. In the emergency room, the doctor suspected that Fran was experiencing a miscarriage. It was not until the next day that they discovered that besides the baby in the uterus, there was also a tubal pregnancy which had resulted in peritonitis. This caused the death not only of both babies but also of Fran. It was her time to depart from this life.

In all the pain, uncertainty, and confusion, Fran had a vivid dream. She was in a large train station filled with expectant people. Looking up, she saw an amazing sight. Coming through the darkened sky was a flying train with windows ablaze with light. The train came to a stop at the platform, and when the doors opened, people started boarding. Fran stood holding onto a column, saying, "I can't leave my children. I can't go yet." That was Fran's last earthly memory.

My first conscious memory of this new life was awakening in a hospital bed, hooked up to machines and experiencing a great deal of pain. I didn't realize that I would be entering a body that was in such physical agony. When the doctor came into my room, he told me that I was lucky to be alive because I had nearly died on the operating table. When the tubes were removed from my throat, I had to learn how to eat. Everything was new to me. I was curious to know what I looked like, but it was a week before I was well enough to walk to the bathroom, where there was a mirror. Imagine what it would be like to see yourself for the first time in a physical body! After several traumatic weeks in the hospital, I was finally strong enough to go *home.*

When Fran's family first came to visit me in the hospital, they were like strangers to me. Because Fran and I had shared past lives with each of the children and her parents, I eventually, began to feel that I was among friends. But for over a year, I was homesick for my Beloved One, my Higher Self. The one I call my Higher Self some may refer to as their Guardian Angel, or the Twin Soul; regardless of the name we use, it is, indeed, our Beloved One.

In the spiritual contract that Fran and I had agreed on, I was to care for her four children and her parents as if they were my own. However, nowhere in the fine print did I see anything about her husband. Because Don was a denying alcoholic and a poor example for the boys, I filed for divorce but did not ask for any financial support. In the judge's office, Don told me I wasn't the same person he had married. How right he was!

For my part, I received a slightly used, thirty-six-year-old body, along with Fran's credentials. She had a college degree in educational psychology and was a tenured teacher for the Los Angeles Board of Education. I also inherited an assortment of duties, including leading a Cub Scout troop and teaching a fourth grade class in the San Fernando Valley. Fran left me most of her memories, but there were a few pieces missing.

I brought with me my spiritual knowledge and psychic abilities, along with a blueprint for an important mission that I chose to accomplish. A part of that mission is to teach classes in parapsychology and to write this book. The purpose of this book is to help you, the reader, to become familiar with and have a better understanding of the next dimension — the World Beyond.

— FranCelia

EXPLORING THE WORLD BEYOND

A Real Astral Adventure

1

Adventuring Around Town

There was an air of excited anticipation as people of all ages and occupations entered the university classroom. I was conducting a class on astral travel at the experimental college of California State University, Northridge.

"Welcome to our class on astral projection. It is my hope," I told the students, "that you come with an open mind and an adventuresome spirit. The purpose of this class is to teach you not only how to travel astrally in the third dimension but also how to consciously explore a land that is not far from here but is invisible to our eyes and shrouded in mystery. Most of the people who go there are not heard from again. Yet every one of us will eventually call it home, because it is the place where we will reside when we leave our physical bodies through death. Some refer to this place as the fourth dimension, the Other Side, the astral world, or the World Beyond. Many religions call it 'Heaven and Hell.'

"The World Beyond is right here, interpenetrating our third-dimensional world. Even though we are sharing the same space, it remains invisible to our physical eyes because it vibrates at such a rapid rate. The astral world has scenery, geography, and buildings just as we have in the physical world. Its inhabitants are just as real as the people of Earth. The difference between the two dimensions is their rate of vibration.

"When we leave the physical world through death, our consciousness will be transferred to our astral body and we will become citizens of the World Beyond. The inhabitants of the astral world include not only those who have left the physical world through death, but also a variety of nature spirits, angelic beings, ghosts, space people, and highly evolved teachers and guides.

"For more than twenty years, I have been able to astrally explore the World Beyond and have become acquainted with some of its inhabitants. In this class, I not only want to give you glimpses into the astral world, but also teach you how to travel there on your own and communicate with the inhabitants of the next dimension. Before we continue, are there any specific questions about astral travel?"

"I've heard the term soul travel. What is the difference between astral projection and soul travel?" asked Eric, an intense young man.

"Astral projection," I replied, "is also known as 'astral travel' or 'mind travel.' Another name is 'out-of-body experience' or OOB. I believe these terms refer to experiences in the third dimension and the lower and middle planes of the astral world, while the term 'soul travel' refers to the experience of traveling in the higher planes of the World Beyond. Because our Soul resides in every cell of our body and cannot travel independently, soul travel is in reality astral travel in a higher vibration."

Melanie, a young girl in the front row, asked, "How can we astrally travel to a specific place?"

"To be successful in reaching a certain place," I answered, "one of three things needs to be present: either you need to know the person you wish to visit so you can be drawn to her by her vibrations; or you need to be familiar with the place you wish to visit; or your Higher Self acts as your guide. With the help of your Higher Self, you can explore the planes of the astral world and visit relatives and friends who are citizens there.

"To learn how to consciously travel astrally," I continued, "it is important to understand that we are multidimensional beings. Besides our physical body, we have an energy or etheric body which interpenetrates the physical body and extends about an inch beyond it. This colorless body is connected to the physical by a short cord at the navel area, and the two remain joined together for life. Our astral or emotional body interpenetrates both the physical and energy body and extends several inches farther. The astral body is connected to the physical at the solar plexus area by a cord composed of an etheral substance that is capable of stretching to the astral world and even to other planets in our solar system. Some have referred to this as the 'silver cord.' It remains attached to the physical body until the Angel of Death severs it and we are set free from the physical world. At that time, the astral body becomes our primary vehicle. And finally, our spiritual or soul body extends about a foot past the astral body and interpenetrates all the other bodies. This is our eternal body — the one that we will inhabit in the Higher Realms."

From the back of the room, Robert said, "This is a completely new concept to me. How can we have all these bodies interpenetrating our physical body?"

"Let me share a story with you," I replied. "It may help to answer your question."

"In a far-away country there once lived a thoughtful young boy. One day the boy went to his mother and asked her a very important question: 'How can bodies that we cannot see dwell within the body that we can see?'

"She told him, 'Son, I don't know the answer to your

question. Why don't you ask your father?'

"The boy went to his father and asked the question. His father said, 'I don't know the answer to your question, but there is a Wise One in the next village who can answer it. When the people ask the Wise One questions, his answers are full of wisdom and truth.'

"That's when the boy decided he must meet the Wise One and ask him this important question. The boy's mother and father agreed to let their son go to the next village. The young boy walked for many hours. Finally, he came to the next village, where he found the Wise One sitting under a big oak tree.

"Many people were standing around the Wise One, asking him questions and listening to his words of wisdom. When the Wise One saw the young boy, he said, 'Come close to me.' The boy made his way past all the people and stood by the Wise One, who asked him, 'Do you have a question that you want answered?'

"'Yes,' the boy replied. 'How can bodies that we cannot see dwell within the body that we can see?'

"The Wise One smiled as he heard the boy's questions. Then he did a very strange thing. He handed a glass jar to the boy and said, 'Go down to the river and fill this jar with stones.' The boy did what he was told: he went down to the river and filled the jar full of smooth, round stones. When he brought the jar back, the Wise One asked, 'Have you filled the jar?'

"'Yes,' the boy replied. 'I filled it to the very top.'

"The Wise One said, 'Go back down to the river and fill the jar of rocks with sand.' So the boy took the jar of stones and went back down to the river. As the boy put sand into the jar, the grains of sand filled the spaces between the rocks. When he brought the jar back, the Wise One asked again, 'Have you filled the jar?'

"'Yes,' replied the boy. 'I have filled it to the very top with rocks and with sand.'

"'Now go down to the river again,' said the Wise One. 'This time fill the jar of rocks and sand with water.' Once more the boy went down to the river. This time he filled the jar of stones and sand with water. When he came back, the Wise One asked, 'Do you now have the answer to your question?'

"With a smile the boy replied, 'You are indeed a very wise man. You have helped me answer my question. Water, sand, and stones are all in the same jar. The water can fill in the spaces between the grains of sand. The sand can fill in the spaces between the stones. Now I understand. The bodies that we cannot see fit between the spaces of the body we can see.'

"Smiling, the Wise One replied, 'Well done, young friend. You are wise beyond your years.'

"So you see," I explained, "the molecules in the physical body are far apart and almost motionless. The molecules in the energy, emotional, and spiritual bodies are composed of increasingly finer substances making it possible for them to fill in the spaces in our physical body. Because they vibrate so rapidly, they are invisible to our physical eyes. As multidimensional beings, each of our bodies is an important part of our total being."

Then I asked the students, "How many of you have had either a conscious or a spontaneous out-of-body experience?"

Several hands were raised, and one woman, Nora, commented, "I know I've astrally projected many times, especially as a child, but I'd like to learn how it is done consciously."

"Astral travel is very common among children," I replied, "because they are free of preconceived ideas and have such wonderful imaginations. Every one of you, whether you are aware of it or not, travels astrally during sleep. With practice, it isn't too difficult to learn to consciously do astral projection. To begin with, we need to learn complete relaxation. When we are relaxed, our physical vibrations slow down. Our breathing becomes shallower and our heart beats more slowly. When our physical body is totally relaxed, we need to quiet our left brain — the analytic mind. Then our right brain — the creative and intuitive mind — will become more aware.

"The nerve cells of our brain send out electrical impulses which can be measured by an electroencephalograph or EEG instrument. When we are concentrating and our mind is active, we send out small, fast impulses called beta waves. When we are relaxed, daydreaming, meditating, or falling asleep, we produce slower waves that repeat from eight to thirteen cycles per second; these are called 'alpha waves.' Conscious astral travel takes place when we are in the alpha state; therefore, the first step in traveling astrally is to enter an altered state of consciousness. You can buy audio tapes that will help you reach the alpha state. However, you may prefer to make your own tape using the method I will use in this class."

Eric asked, "What does it feel like to be in the alpha state?"

"To me, it's a detached, slowing down, peaceful feeling," I replied. "It's the feeling you get when you are on the verge of going to sleep, yet at the same time, a part of you feels centered and alert. Sometimes when your astral body leaves the physical body there may be a sense of weightlessness, as if you're floating. While in the astral body, you will probably feel a sense of freedom. Most people experience dual consciousness — that is, feeling equally cognizant of the physical body and the sensations of the astral body. This is natural and will become less pronounced as you become more adept at astral travel. The astral body can travel with the speed of thought: simply desire to be in a certain place or with a certain person, and you are there. With practice, you will be able to go anywhere you desire.

"Before taking off, always remember to fasten your spiritual seat belt by visualizing the White Light of protection coming from your Higher Self and completely surrounding you. Now nothing can harm you. You cannot fall or hurt yourself. You cannot get lost, because your astral and physical body are connected by a cord that is marvelously strong and elastic.

"If at any time you are startled by a sound or you become afraid, you will immediately return to your physical body. If you should happen to fall asleep while traveling astrally, it's no problem, because when you wake up you will be back in your physical body. When you are ready to return to your physical body, merely *think* that you are going back. There will be an instantaneous shift from wherever you were astrally back to your physical body. Your breathing and heartbeat will then return to normal.

"All right, class, we are ready to take an astral trip. For our first adventure, we're going to travel right here in our own neighborhood." Several students had brought pillows and mats to class, so they arranged themselves on the floor. Some chose to sit on the floor and lean against the wall, while the others remained in their seats. After dimming the lights and instructing the students to settle themselves in a comfortable position, I began in a slow, soothing voice: "Relax ... your eyes are closed ... relax ... relax all over ... yawn a couple of times ... with each breath that you take you are going deeper and deeper into the alpha state ... relax your feet ... relax your legs ... relax your hips

... let all the tension leave your body ... relax your hands ... relax your arms. If you have any worries, problems, or concerns, visualize them in a ball on your shoulders. Now, see that ball rolling off your shoulders and out the door, freeing you of all problems, concerns, and worries. Now relax your shoulders ... relax your neck muscles ... relax your facial muscles ... you are now completely relaxed.

"Now visualize a celestial escalator moving slowly upward ... ready ... step on ... as you move upward, your vibrations are raised higher and higher ... one, two higher and higher; three, four higher and higher" (as I count, my voice becomes slower and softer); "five, six higher and higher; seven, eight higher and higher; nine, ten higher and higher; eleven, twelve higher and higher; thirteen, fourteen higher and higher; fifteen, sixteen higher and higher; seventeen, eighteen higher and higher; nineteen, twenty ... stepping off the escalator.

"Now, visualize a beautiful stream of white light coming from your Higher Self. Let that light enter your crown center at the top of your head and flow to every part of your body ... bringing peace and relaxation. Now visualize your astral body standing in front of you. It looks very much like you. Feel yourself floating upward. Picture the roof opening up, making it possible for you to float up into the air above the campus. Now I want you to astrally go home the way you came to class. When you arrive, look around. Observe what is happening. Are there people in your home? Become aware of the sights and sounds around you."

We sat in complete silence for some time until I said softly, "It is now time to return to your physical body. You will feel completely at ease and rested. You are filled with a deep, relaxing peace. You will remember everything that you saw, heard, and experienced. It will be clear in your mind. As I count from three to one, you will return to your physical body. Three ... awake, alert, and aware! Two ... awake, alert, and aware! One ... awake, alert and aware! You may open your eyes when you are ready."

For a few minutes we sat quietly. Then, one by one, each student was given an opportunity to share his or her experience with the rest of the group. One man had gone so deeply into the alpha state that he had fallen asleep. He had consciously missed the whole trip. Several women said they had only fleeting glimpses of the World Beyond but that they saw bursts of brilliant colors. The rest of the group were excited about their experiences in the astral world. They each saw and heard with various degrees of clarity and accuracy. As a group, this was a typical reaction to a first-time adventure.

Over the years that I have been teaching astral travel, I have discovered that sometimes students are unsuccessful because they try too hard. I tell my students to approach astral travel with a childlike faith and a certain amount of carefreeness. Some people expect to see as clearly with their astral sight as they do with their physical eyes. They don't realize that as they watch an astral scene, it may fluctuate or even disappear. Then there are some people who just need more practice than others to be able to travel astrally.

At the beginning of our second class, I asked, "Are there any questions or comments about our experience last week?" In almost every class that I taught at the university, there were usually one or two nonbelievers. They seemed to enjoy sharing their doubts and disbelief with the other students. I felt that Ron was one of these doubters, so I was surprised when he said that he had something he wanted to share with the other students.

Ron told the class, "Last week when you helped us get into a meditative state, I got into what I considered a deep state but I didn't seem to achieve any significant astral experience. After the class was over, I drove home in my pickup truck. When I walked into the house, my wife asked me why I had come home earlier that evening and then left again. I asked her what she meant, and she explained that about eight o'clock that night she had heard my truck pull into the driveway and stop. She hadn't heard me drive away and she wondered why I didn't come into the house. My son was playing in a neighbor's yard where the view of our house was partially obscured by bushes. He saw my truck drive up and pull into our long driveway out of his sight. Then he heard the engine turn off. Later when he came into the house, he asked his mother where I was. He couldn't understand why I wasn't home because he hadn't seen or heard me leave.

"As near as I can calculate," Ron continued, "we were practicing astral travel at the same time my wife and son heard my truck pull into our driveway ten miles from the college campus. Evidently, I took the instruction you gave literally when you said to go home the way we usually do. I believe I did travel astrally, even though I had no knowledge of the experience myself."

Many people find it difficult to visualize existence in any body but the physical, and the idea of having an out-of-body experience seems improbable to them. Like Ron, they will probably need a personal experience to convert them into believers.

After Ron had shared his experience, I told the class, "Tonight we are going to learn how to take a mini-vacation. I've found that one of the most rewarding outcomes of learning to travel astrally is the ability to experience a mini-vacation. In a few minutes, you can feel as refreshed as if you'd been resting for a long time. When I come home exhausted after teaching school all day, I often settle myself in a comfortable bedroom chair, relax my body, quiet my mind, and enjoy an astral mini-vacation. One evening when I was astrally sitting on the shore of a beautiful lake, I was startled by a scream. My daughter had come into my bedroom and thought I was dead. The physical body looks inanimate when the emotional — or astral — body is out exploring. I learned that day to lock my bedroom door before leaving on a mini-vacation.

"Now I want each of you to think of a special place that you would enjoy visiting astrally," I continued. "It could be at the seashore, by a cascading mountain stream, in a forest glen, or in a special place from your childhood. To take a mini-vacation, settle yourself in a comfortable position, either sitting or lying down. Quietly relax. Close your eyes and enter the alpha state. Then visualize your special place. Now feel yourself there. Use all of your astral senses to enjoy the experience. When you return from your mini-vacation, you will probably feel not only rested but also filled with a deep sense of peace."

After the students had been astrally experiencing a mini-vacation for about ten minutes, I said softly, "It is time to return. As I count from three to one you will be back in your physical body. Three ... awake ... alert ... aware! Two, awake, alert, aware! One, awake, alert, aware!"

The students were again given an opportunity to share their experiences. One of the most interesting was the one Florence shared with the class. Florence told us, "I decided to astrally visit the home of my childhood. As I astrally walked into the living room, I was absolutely amazed! Everything looked exactly as I remembered it when I was living there in my early teens, over ten years ago: the same rug, the same furniture — even my piano. All these things were sold or given away when we moved, and yet here they were, still existing in the astral world. How can this be?"

"The conventional idea of time is obviously inadequate when we are exploring astrally," I explained. "In the physical world, we have linear time. We can remember the past; we are living in the present; we can only guess what the future holds in store for us. In the next dimension, time still relates to the Earth plane, but it is also governed by the Celestial World where time is experienced as the Eternal Now. Each of us has stored our past experiences in our memory bank. Therefore, our experiences still exist — perhaps not in a physical reality, but in some dimension of their own."

After everyone had an opportunity to share experiences, I told the class, "This week I have a homework assignment for you. I want you to practice traveling astrally on your own. You wouldn't expect to sit down and play a piano concerto at a recital without a great deal of practice. It takes practice to play a good game of golf or to produce a beautiful oil painting. Yet we are often frustrated and disappointed if we can't travel astrally on the first or second time we make the attempt. It does take practice to learn how to achieve an altered state of consciousness. It does take practice to get used to the higher frequencies and to be able to use our astral senses. However, with patience and practice, it is possible to see and hear clearly in the next dimension. With practice, it is possible to leave your physical body and go exploring in your astral body.

"When you're ready to practice a solo astral flight,

choose a time and place where you will have no outside distractions. Make sure that the phone is disconnected and that your pets or family members are not going to disturb you. Lie down on your back with your legs straight and your arms comfortably at your sides. It's wise to cover yourself with a blanket as the physical body sometimes becomes cold during an astral trip. When you're settled, close your eyes, relax, and breathe slowly. To be successful, complete relaxation of the body and mind is required. You need to quiet your rational left brain while your intuitive right brain remains alert and aware. You accomplish this by entering an altered state of consciousness.

"Each of you needs to discover the best method to use in order to achieve the alpha state. Perhaps it may be by listening to a training tape that has been created especially to teach astral projection, or by listening to a tape that you have made, patterned after the example I used in our first class. With practice, you may be able to enter the alpha state simply by counting slowly from one to twenty as you visualize walking up a flight of stairs or ascending in an elevator or escalator. As you become more experienced, you may be able to achieve the alpha state simply by closing your eyes and relaxing. The more you practice, the easier it becomes to enter an altered state of consciousness.

"Once you have achieved the altered state, imagine yourself lying in a hammock, gently rocking back and forth. Now gradually feel the hammock lift you higher off the bed. Picture yourself putting your feet over the edge of the hammock and standing up. Imagine yourself walking around the room. Explore the ceiling and other places in the room where you would not normally be able to go. You will discover that you can walk through walls or go up through the ceiling with little or no effort.

"As you become more adventuresome, you may

decide to visit a neighbor or friend. Suggestion plays an important part in astral projection. Visualize the person or place you wish to visit. Imagine yourself already being there. Let a desire build up in you for this astral journey. Have complete faith and confidence in your ability to reach your objective. Because time and space are different in the fourth dimension, it is possible to travel instantaneously to any distant place you choose with merely a thought.

"When you're ready to return from your astral exploration, think of yourself lying on the bed. As you're thinking this, you may experience a drifting toward your body or a sudden sinking downward into your physical body. With practice and the help of your Higher Self, you will be able to explore Earth and even the planes of the World Beyond."

After I had explained the homework assignment to practice astral travel on their own, I told the students, "Next week we are going to take our first trip to the World Beyond. Please bring a pillow and either a blanket or sleeping bag so your physical body will be comfortable while we are out exploring. I'll see you next week!"

2

Spontaneous Astral Projection

Whether we are aware of it or not, every one of us has experiences spontaneous astral projection while sleeping. It is a natural occurrence. Most of us, however, don't remember our astral adventures when we awaken. While out-of-body, some people may stay in their own neighborhood, while others are out traveling far and wide. Some may be merely enjoying a little outing, while others are helping someone in need or attending a lecture at an astral university.

Our sleep state goes in cycles throughout the night, from light alpha to a very deep state and then back to light alpha. It's during this deepest sleep state, when our physical body is relatively still, that we travel astrally. It is then that we are able to astrally visit our loved ones who have left the physical world through death. We can also spend time with our Higher Self, our Guardian Angel.

I believe that during sleep we experience several different types of dreams. One I call a "junk dream" because it is of little or no value. It may be concerned with something we are worrying about, going over and over the same thought. Perhaps it was inspired by a movie or a television show we just saw. Another type of dream I refer to as a "training film" because it relays valuable information to us from our Higher Self. Then there is another type that may seem like a dream but in reality is an actual out-of-body experience. If you have ever dreamed that you were flying or running or falling, you were probably tuning in to an out-of-body experience. People who walk in their sleep may be going one step farther by taking their physical bodies along with them as they travel astrally.

To remember and learn from our dreams, we need to record them as soon as possible. It's wise to keep paper and pencil by your bed. Before you go to sleep, ask your Higher Self to help you remember your dream and to be able to know whether it was an actual astral experience. A dream is usually a symbolic occurrence: actors and scenery are often out of proportion and exaggerated, while the sensation of astral travel seems very real. Everything appears just as though you were viewing it with your physical eyes. With practice, you will be able to discern the difference between a dream and an out-of-body experience.

We can help our children have pleasant dreams at naptime or bedtime by guiding them on a little astral trip. This is also a good way to settle children down and prepare them for sleep. Most youngsters are naturally adept at astral travel. Speak slowly and softly to them as you guide their thoughts on a fantasy trip. Young children love to go to a fairyland, while older ones enjoy visiting faraway places. They will probably fall asleep while they are traveling — and that's fine, because when they awaken they will be back in their physical body.

While asleep, we can also attend an astral university to hear a lecture on a topic that interests us. Time in the astral world is not the same as in the physical world. It is possible to hear a whole lecture, while in the physical world only a few minutes elapse. All that we learn or experience while traveling astrally is stored in our subconscious mind (the memory) even though our conscious mind may not be aware of the information. Later, something that we read or hear may trigger that memory, causing our conscious mind to become aware of the information. We may wonder why the information seems so familiar because we didn't realize that it had been stored in our subconscious mind.

During our sleep, healing can occur. If we are feeling ill or tired, we can ask our Higher Self to send us healing energy. Astral doctors are available, and they still make house calls. I have felt astral hands as they adjust my spine or ease my physical pain. At other times, we may be taken to a healing center where our astral body is strengthened and healed with the use of light and sound. Having a healthy astral body is very important because it directly affects the well-being of our physical body.

Sometimes during our sleep, we may be called upon to astrally help someone make the transition into the World Beyond. Many times I have been asked to go to a fatal accident to give comfort and confidence to someone who has died. One of my first experiences occurred many years ago when a passenger jet and a small plane collided over San Diego. There was such confusion! People were running around carrying parts of their bodies, not realizing that they were no longer physically alive. I approached a distraught woman and was finally able to quiet her fears and escort her into the World Beyond, but it was a very traumatic experience.

About a year later, again while asleep, I was asked to go astrally to help victims of another plane crash. This time it was quite different. The plane was just taking off from O'Hare Airport in Chicago when it crashed and burned. When I astrally arrived at the crash scene, there was no panic, because everyone had died so suddenly. The passengers, with the help of the stewardesses, were boarding several astral buses in an orderly manner. They seemed unaware of the fact that they were dead, and everyone was quite calm. To my surprise, nobody needed my help.

As we near the end of this century, Earth will experience an increasing number of natural and manmade catastrophes. We who have chosen to be of service to others will have many opportunities to help people make their transition, through death, into the next dimension. Some of you may already be astrally helping, although you may not be consciously aware of your activities. If you wish to volunteer, intuitively let your Higher Self know of your decision. You may also ask to remember your nightly rescue work. When you are called on to help astrally in an emergency, remember that you are not alone. Your Higher Self, your partner, will be by your side instructing you in the ways you can help.

It is important that we always awaken slowly and gently, because our astral body may be out somewhere adventuring, and we need to allow the astral and physical bodies time to become aligned. The shrill sound of an alarm clock or a loud clock radio can startle us causing the astral body to be drawn back to the physical body with a jolt. It helps if we take a few minutes to stretch our arms, legs, and spine before hopping out of bed. We also need to be careful how we awaken others, especially children. Shaking or using a loud voice can cause their astral bodies to return to their physical bodies so quickly that they may feel shocked or confused for a few minutes.

Most of us experience spontaneous astral travel while we are asleep; however, there are other instances when we may leave our physical bodies. A spontaneous astral projection can occur during a time of crisis, or while we are unconscious because of illness or injury. There are those who report that while under an anesthetic, they found themselves floating above the operating table, where they could see and hear the doctors and nurses.

A friend of mine told of her amazing astral experience during an operation. "I remember being wheeled into the operating room for breast surgery. The next thing I knew, I was floating above my body, looking down and seeing and hearing everything that was going on. Then beside me appeared my mother, who had died several years before. She had a happy expression on her face, as though she was glad to see me. I thought I must be having a vivid dream. When I looked down, I saw that the doctor was greatly concerned. I heard the nurse tell him that she felt no pulse, and then I saw the doctor making a frenzied effort to resuscitate me.

"Although I was somewhat dazed and confused, I felt a curious sense of detachment as I viewed the scene below me. Then my mother took my arm and started to lead me away. A shocking realization hit me. I must be dead! I pulled away and exclaimed, 'No, I can't go with you. I can't leave my children. I can't die now!' I realized that I must somehow return to my physical body.

"The instant I made that decision I found myself back in my physical body. Then I heard the doctor say, 'She's coming to.' The doctor was astounded when I told him what I had seen and heard while under the anesthetic."

Ever since I read the following escape story involving spontaneous astral travel, it has intrigued me. Around the turn of the twentieth century, Ed Morrel was sentenced to a four-year term in the Arizona State Prison, which had the reputation of being a real hell hole. Sadistic guards practiced cruel and inhuman punishment. One day Morrel was punished by being placed in a double straitjacket made of buckskin and doused with water. The pain caused by the shrinking buckskin was unbearable. Hour after hour, Morrel was left in this state. The next day, when the guards finally returned to his cell, they found — much to their disbelief — that the prisoner was asleep and smiling.

After Morrel was released from prison, he related, "I suffered for about half an hour. Then a warm feeling descended over my body. I felt at peace. I found myself in the outside world, roaming freely wherever I wished to go." Events that he said he had witnessed outside the prison were carefully checked out and found to be as he had described them. Remarkably, through astral travel, Morrel was able to escape the pain of his imprisonment.

For several years, I worked as a volunteer at a nursing home. Even the best nursing home is not an easy place in which to live or work. However, from their blank stares and unresponsiveness, I soon realized that many of the patients had astrally escaped the nursing home, leaving behind their physical bodies. How lucky for them that even though their physical body still existed in the third dimension, they were able to spend some time enjoying life in the World Beyond!

Spontaneous astral projection can also result from a drug overdose or the influence of alcohol. Many years ago, my Higher Self led me to a young girl who was experiencing a bad reaction to a drug overdose. She was wandering around trying to find her way back to her physical body.

She was really frightened because she didn't understand what was happening. Together we followed the astral cord back to her physical body. Her hair and clothes were disheveled and covered with vomit, and it took me quite awhile to persuade the girl to get back into her body. Finally she agreed after I promised to stay with her until someone arrived to take care of her.

Sometimes when a patient is in a coma, his consciousness wavers back and forth from the physical to the astral world. Doctors and nurses relate that when patients regain consciousness, they often tell of meeting friends and relatives who are already on the Other Side. As death draws near, this experience can bring them a sense of peace.

There are thousands of accounts from people who report that they left their physical bodies during a time when they were critically ill or injured and thought to be dying. They tell of visiting distant places or loved ones, on both this side and the other side of life. While having a near death experience, many said they found themselves in an environment of such beauty and peace that they were reluctant to return to their physical bodies. As a consequence of their experience, they stated that they would never again fear death. As more and more near-death experiences are reported, we are being given revealing glimpses into the next dimension.

Researchers have been working on ways to test people's ability to travel astrally. One method is to observe a sleeping subject and monitor his brain waves. The target for the experiment is a picture placed in such a way that the subject can see it only if he is able to travel astrally. The subject is awakened when the researchers determine by the brain waves that he has completed the deep sleep cycle.

The subject is then questioned to see if he has seen the target picture.

In ancient Egypt they had a foolproof way of testing to see whether a person could leave his physical body and travel astrally. One women I knew passed that test but lost her life in the process.

While I was living in the San Fernando Valley, Louise, the principal of an elementary school, came to me for a past-life regression. She told me of her tremendous fear of death — not only her own death, but also that of her friends and family. She felt that a regression would help her understand this phobia.

The life that Louise relived took place in ancient Egypt. She was going through one of the last initiations towards mastership. This was a test to see if the person really could get out of the body and travel astrally. She was placed in a sarcophagus and the heavy lid was put on top. There she was to remain for three days. If she was unable to astrally leave her physical body, she would surely die. She was successful in astrally escaping the tomb, but at the end of the three days, when she returned to her physical body, something went wrong. The priest who had the responsibility of staying by her side during this initiation was in a drunken stupor and did not lift the lid off the sarcophagus, so she died a frightening death. Since then, life after life, Louise has carried this fear of death with her. However, after understanding the source of her fear, she was better able to cope with her phobia.

The concept that we possess an astral body which is a replica of our physical body but made of a more ethereal substance can be traced back to the Greeks. Aristotle theorized that the human soul occupies a body which resembles the substance of the stars — hence the name "astral," which means "starry." However, a more accurate name would be the "emotional body," because it is so closely connected with our emotions.

Our astral body interpenetrates the physical body and extends beyond it for several inches. The portion of the astral body that extends beyond the physical body is often referred to as the "aura." The aura is composed of a fluctuating array of colors. These colors are affected not only by our emotions but also by our thoughts, health, intellect, and spirituality. The aura is always moving and the colors are constantly melding into one another. The various colors sometimes disappear, only to return later. The more spiritual a person is, the clearer and richer the colors appear. People who are not on the spiritual path have duller auras. Illness and depression produce gray overtones in the aura. After a sudden shock, the colors fade out and the whole emotional body takes on a grayish hue. The aura reacts immediately to our emotions: a sudden rush of emotion can flood the aura with a different color that pertains to the particular emotion being experienced. For example, intense anger produces black with streaks of red; jealousy has a greenish-brown hue; fear is gray; devotion is blue; pride is orange; and, of course, true love is pink.

I have learned a great deal about the astral body from my grandma. How well I remember my surprise the first time I astrally visited her in the World Beyond. She appeared much as I remembered her — short and plump, with her gray hair pulled back in a little bun. "Would you like to see where I've been working?" Grandma asked, after she had given me a loving hug.

"Of course," I answered, eager to learn all I could about the Other Side.

Grandma led me inside a large, modern building to a room where several old ladies were sitting in wheelchairs knitting. Their faces were expressionless, and they appeared more dead than alive. Impatiently, I said to these women, "Don't you know that you can get up and walk? You're in Heaven, where nobody needs to be sick or crippled!" But they seemed unmoved by my impetuous outburst.

Grandma didn't scold me but said softly, "Nobody can change another person's mind for them. It takes some people longer than others to realize that they are no longer in a physical body. Let's go outside. I'd like to show you the real me."

Startled by this statement, I followed her into a little garden outside the building. There before my astral eyes, I saw my grandmother transformed into a beautiful, petite woman who appeared to be in her mid-twenties. She gracefully twirled around so I could get the full impact of her metamorphosis. "This is the real me," she said, "but I knew that you wouldn't have recognized me this way, so I became as you remembered me on Earth. Here we become the age that we want to be. Many people choose to be eternally young, while some choose to be more advanced in years. It depends on the person and what age on Earth they were the most successful and productive. I personally enjoy being young!"

Grandma continued, "Our astral bodies are affected entirely by mind power, and so we can look any way we wish. At first, it seems more natural to appear exactly as we did when we died, no matter how old or miserable we might have been. As soon as we learn how to control our thoughts, we can become as young and as beautiful or handsome as we desire. Some of the people here have beards, and others are clean-shaven. We have people who have long, curly hair, and people who are bald. If we want to change our appearance, we simply think it into being. Our bodies are as real and solid to us here in the astral world as your physical bodies are to you on Earth. However, we are invisible to the physical eye because we are vibrating at a much higher frequency."

It was time for me to return to my physical body, so I gave my young grandma a big hug, and in a split second I was back in my physical body.

Just as the physical body is composed of solids, liquids, and gases, so too is the astral body. Solid physical matter is interpenetrated by solid astral matter; liquid physical by liquid astral; and physical gas by astral gas. Because astral matter is much finer than physical matter, an astral person might be occupying the same space as a physical person, yet each would be completely unaware of the other.

If a person's leg, arm, or other body part is amputated, its astral counterpart remains and retains its original shape. This may account for the phantom pain that is so often reported by amputees. The astral body may, in some way not yet understood, feel pain even though the physical counterpart is missing. A friend of mine who had his leg amputated above the knee especially enjoys astral travel, because then he can walk and run on his astral legs.

Just as we have five physical senses, we also possess five astral senses which operate in the next dimension. These astral senses are usually referred to as ESP (Extra Sensory Perception), or the "sixth sense." To use this sixth sense, it is necessary to be in an altered state of consciousness. Some call this a hypnotic state, a light trance, or the alpha state.

The astral sense of sight is believed to be connected

with the third eye. Cosmic wisdom tells us that the third eye is located in the pineal gland, which is near the center of the brain, though it is not a part of the brain. The pineal gland is the size of a pea and is shaped like a pine cone, hence its name. This gland also acts like a biological clock. It secretes a different amount of certain chemicals during periods of light or during darkness. This increases bodily activity and temperature during the day and decreases them at night.

By using the astral sense of sight we can — among other things — see through solid physical objects and see behind as easily as we can see in front, giving us 360° vision. When observing in the astral planes, it is important that we are aware that things will appear to fluctuate, change, and even disappear as we watch them.

The pineal gland is also thought to be an "inner ear." The astral sense of hearing (called "clairaudience") allows us to tune in to our friends and relatives in the World Beyond, as well as to the Masters and our own beloved Higher Self. The astral sense of feeling may be best defined as intuition (called "clairvoyance"). We seldom use the astral senses of taste and smell.

Often the senses are enhanced during an out-of-body experience. Many report that while traveling in their astral bodies they feel more alert and observant. Others experience a heightened sense of elation and a greater depth of emotion. I've often been moved to tears of pure joy while astrally visiting the higher planes because the vibrations of love there are so powerful.

Although we have little or no control over spontaneous astral projections, we can ask our Higher Self to help us become more aware of them, whether they occur while we are asleep, during a crisis, under an anesthetic, or when we are in a coma or near death. Now is the time for us to remember our spontaneous, out-of-body adventures, as well as to experience conscious astral travel.

3

Exploring the Middle Astral

By our third class on astral travel, the skeptics and the curious had dropped out. Now the remaining students and I could bond in a special way. Together we were beginning our astral adventure — exploring the World Beyond. The students came into the classroom carrying pillows and blankets or sleeping bags, which they arranged comfortably on the floor.

"Before beginning tonight's exploration," I explained, "let's take an imaginary tour of one of our larger cities here in the United States to give us a better understanding of the different sections of the astral world. As we approach the city, we see out of our car window the poorer section of town — the slum area. There are numerous bars and tenement houses sadly in need of repair. Graffiti cover the walls and trash litters the streets. As we drive along, the atmosphere gradually changes and we begin to see neighborhoods of family houses, schools, and shopping centers. The homes and yards look well-kept and neighborhood children are playing together.

"As we continue our tour, we come to the most beautiful part of the town. Large homes are set in tranquil, parklike settings. There are many open spaces with golf courses, playgrounds, and lakes. We are impressed by the beauty we see here. The company that we work for is transferring our family and will furnish us a place to live, rent free. We are all hoping that we will be able to move into one of these mansions.

"To determine the neighborhood and home we will be assigned, we are told we must pass through a very sensitive machine that will indicate only one thing: the depth of our spiritual love. This really surprises us, because we thought the company would take into consideration how hard we had worked for them. After we pass through the machine, which looks very much like a metal detector at the airport, we anxiously wait to see where we will be living.

"Where we will dwell when we enter the World Beyond through death will not be determined by how famous we are, or how much we have accomplished in our physical life, or whether we belong to a certain religious group, but by the degree of our spiritual love. True spiritual love is unconditional and nonjudgmental. The greater our love, the higher our vibrations. When we leave the physical world through death and enter the astral world, we will find ourselves in a place that matches our own vibrations and spiritual evolvement.

"The World Beyond has distinct planes of existence. Each level has its own unique frequency or rate of vibration. For convenience, I have divided the astral planes into three groups: the lower planes, the middle planes, and the higher planes. We can explore any of these different planes when we travel astrally.

"Tonight, I have chosen for our destination the middle astral planes, because they will not be such a culture shock as the lower planes. In fact, the middle astral looks very much like our physical world. Now, as you become comfortable, close your eyes, relax, and breathe deeply." In a quiet voice, I led the students into the alpha state. Then

I told them, "Now visualize yourself entering a celestial elevator. The doors are closing and the elevator is going up ... up ... up."

When the elevator doors open, we are greeted with a sight very much like one we would expect to see back home on Earth. We see a modern city where people are rushing around carrying on business as usual. In fact, everything seems so normal that some new arrivals are not even aware that they have entered the next dimension. Here they continue living in the same way and doing the same things they did in the physical world, until they finally realize that they are in another phase of life. This realization may take days, months, or even years.

Here in the middle planes there are residential and commercial areas where the houses and places of business look like those of Earth, constructed of material that resembles wood, brick, or stucco. To the astral citizens, their world is as real as the physical world is for us.

There is a great variety in character and occupations in the middle astral planes. Everyone seems to be busy — working at a chosen career, taking classes at one of the many universities, or enjoying a favorite kind of recreation. After communicating with many newly arrived citizens in the astral world, I find that working with flowers is a good way for many of them to adjust to their new life in the World Beyond.

The inhabitants of the middle astral planes have the opportunity to work out the intellectual and creative aspirations that they were unable to fulfill or complete on Earth. Artists paint masterpieces; musicians create great compositions; architects build beautiful buildings; inventors discover new things. Each experiences the joy of using his or her creative imagination. Astral material is shaped by the thoughts and imaginative powers of the minds of those inhabiting these planes. Often, the blueprints for the works of art, musical compositions, great literature, and inventions conceived here are telepathically channeled to people living on Earth.

There are a variety of schools and universities here. Classes offer an endless choice of subjects, making it possible for people to pursue their personal interests. These astral universities are filled with students of all ages. Earth people may also attend these schools in their astral body, usually during the sleep state.

In the middle planes, each of the great religions has its own particular place where people with like beliefs can gather to worship. All forms of religion — ancient and modern, Eastern and Western — are represented here. Beautiful temples, churches, and cathedrals provide each religious group with a place of worship.

Marriage as we know it on Earth does not exist in the next dimension. However, a couple may choose to remain together as long as they desire. My father died several years before my mother, and he prepared a home for the two of them that was almost identical to their home on Earth. They have been happily together for many years on the Other Side. The time may come, however, when they will feel comfortable going their separate ways, until their paths again cross in another place and another time.

Those who have had a marriage based only on sex, or who have stayed together because of a sense duty to their children, probably will not remain together for very long in the World Beyond. Some couples feel, because of their religious beliefs, that they are bound to each other for all eternity; and they are, until they realize that they are now free of the marriage vows of the physical plane.

If a person has had more than one marriage partner, the one closer in vibrational compatibility will probably remain with the mate. If a couple, married or not, have experienced a deep, abiding love for each other on Earth, they will most likely find their relationship enhanced in the next world and will continue evolving together. Remember that people's vibrations are dependent on their capacity to give unconditional and nonjudgmental love.

All family members have their own individual spiritual vibrations. If the difference is slight, they may continue to live together as a family unit as each enters the World Beyond through physical death. If some are incompatible, they will have little attraction for the rest of the family unit. When family members are separated, the lower-plane dweller may visit the higher plane but cannot remain there too long because of the vibrational differences. While visiting a higher plane, the astral person must raise his vibrations, but before long the gravitational pull of his own level calls him back. Those on the higher planes have the ability to adjust their body's vibration rate to a lower level, but soon they too are attracted back to their own plane. Gradually the tie that bound these people together on Earth, whether through marriage or birth, will be broken. Then they will be free to let go of the relationship and go their separate ways.

Some unaware astral citizens wear the clothes they have always worn. Others who are more aware understand how to use their creative thought power and can mentally create any costume they desire. Sometimes those who have been in the military continue to wear their uniforms as a matter of pride. Charles, a handsome Marine I had known and loved, was killed while fighting in Korea. The following is one of his channeled messages to me:

> *Dear Fran, I'm still proud of being a Marine. I often wear my Marine Corps uniform and this gives reassurance to those I am trying to help. It is good that many of our men who died in battle have received medals posthumously. They are very proud of them and mentally create duplicates so they can wear their medals up here. I have been working with the men who have died in the Vietnam War. I have found great satisfaction in helping them make the transition between Earth and Heaven with the least possible trauma. What a comfort it is to have someone take you by the hand and lead you up and away.*
>
> *Often, loving spirit women go to the battlefields of the world and cradle the heads of the dead and dying in their laps as they speak words of comfort and assurance. This is a great help, for so many of the boys are very young. It is like having their own mother's love with them at this final moment of their Earth's existence. Some of the dying need a male spirit's strong arm to lean on; some need a female spirit's loving care. We somehow know which type of help is needed.*
>
> *I have often sat and had long talks with the men after they have come over, because they don't seem to want to sleep or rest but are very curious about what has happened and what is going to happen. Time and time again they ask, "Where are we anyway? Why are we here?" We are so much the same as we were on Earth. The change is primarily in our awareness. We begin to realize that there are many truths about life and death*

that we had not even been aware of on Earth. My love to you, Charles.

There are many hospitals and healing centers in the World Beyond. Doctors in every field of medicine are working to discover new and better methods of curing disease. Science is very important in the World Beyond. There are many laboratories staffed with astral scientists who are working diligently to find solutions for the problems of Earth. Once a discovery has been made, this information is telepathically sent to doctors and scientists on Earth. Because of this, a new medical or scientific breakthrough is often discovered by several Earth scientists at the same time.

When someone has experienced a lingering or difficult death, he is taken to an astral hospital where he can be helped to make a better adjustment to his new home. When my father died at ninety-three, he had just broken his hip in a fall from a ladder. The first time I visited him on the Other Side, he was sitting in a wheelchair in a rest home that looked like an expensive vacation resort. He knew he had passed over, and he was enjoying all the attention he was receiving from the attractive nurses. He was soon able to go to his own home, but others may take a much longer time to adjust. They are unaware that their astral bodies are not subject to illness or disease as were their physical bodies. Although illness as we understand it in the physical world does not exist, the astral hospitals and rest homes are filled with patients who seem to be experiencing every ailment imaginable. Patients needing treatment are taken into cubicles where sound and light are used to restore their astral cells. In this way, astral physicians and nurses are able to work directly with the individual patient's vibratory pattern.

Food in the astral world may be either required, optional, or unnecessary. For those who are unaware that they exist in a new dimension, food seems to be required for sustenance. They eat the same food that they were accustomed to eating during their Earth lives. It often tastes even more delicious, though, because their astral taste buds have a keener sensitivity.

The optional consumption of food is usually a social activity. Some people are aware that their bodies are sustained by astral energies, but they enjoy an occasional banquet with friends. If you have ever dreamed of attending a feast or sharing a meal with friends or family on the Other Side, you were probably enjoying a festive celebration in the World Beyond. Food, however, is not necessary to sustain the astral body.

In the middle planes, people use many different kinds of transportation; from cars and trams much like those in Disneyland to spacecraft. A more efficient method of travel, though, is through thought power. By visualizing the location and desiring to be there, people who are aware of their ability can instantaneously visit any place they wish.

Sex in the middle planes is different than what we experience in the physical world. Sexual expression, or spiritual love, occurs easily — by a glance, by touching fingertips, or by *going all the way.* The last can be best described as a heartfelt hug in which all the centers are aligned. This sexual activity is not one of passion, but rather a revitalizing energy for the participants — if the individuals involved have a compatible, harmonious vibration.

Animals and plants are also drawn to the part of the astral plane that matches their vibrations. Of course, this applies to the nature spirits as well. In the middle regions and in the children's Heaven, I have often seen deer, rabbits, and a variety of birds and butterflies. Farm animals and household pets are also found on the middle astral planes.

Our tour group had not planned to visit the children's Heaven, which is a special place in the middle astral planes. While some members of our group wandered off to explore on their own, I shared with several of the students my personal experience of visiting the children's Heaven.

My first visit to the children's Heaven came unexpectedly, one hot August afternoon in 1973. I had been catching up on my housecleaning when suddenly I became so exhausted that I felt that I just had to lie down for awhile. As soon as I stretched out on my bed and relaxed, I experienced a strange, detached, floating sensation as my astral body left my physical body. The next moment I found myself astrally in the midst of an accident. I could see red lights flashing and hear the wail of sirens in the distance. There was so much confusion! Police and firemen were rushing about between the jumble of cars and rescue equipment.

Suddenly my attention was drawn to a little boy who was clinging to his mother as she lay on a stretcher that was being loaded into an ambulance. No one seemed aware of the child. Somehow I knew that I should help this boy. I took his hand and led him away from the wreckage. As we sat down on some grass, great sobs shook him, and I put my arms around the child to comfort him. "What's your name?" I asked to get his attention.

In a very small, tearful voice he said, "Bobby."

"How old are you, Bobby?" I asked. He held up

three fingers. "I like children," I continued, as I gave him a loving hug.

Gradually he stopped crying. Then he looked at me and asked, "Why are you wearing such funny clothes?"

Looking down, I found that I was astrally wearing the same old, mismatched clothes I had on physically. "I left in a hurry," I told him, "I didn't have time to change."

As we sat quietly, I realized that the boy had died in the accident, so I asked him, "Have you heard about Heaven?" He just nodded. "Would you like to go there with me?" Again there was just a tearful nod. So taking his hand lovingly in mine, I astrally left the scene of the accident, and in what seemed only a moment we were in the children's Heaven.

We stood there for a few minutes, just looking around. The air was filled with the sound of children's laughter. Some of the youngsters were swinging, while others were playing games together. Several girls were wading in a little stream that flowed gently through the playground. Puppies, kittens, and rabbits happily mingled with the youngsters. A group of school-age children were sitting on the grass, listening intently to their teacher. As I watched the children, they all seemed busy, healthy, and happy. Soon a young spirit woman came over to us, and I told her, "This is Bobby, and he has just arrived."

"You will be very happy here in your new home, Bobby," she said, taking his other hand. Together we entered a long one-story building. "He is very tired," the young woman said to me. "I think he would like to rest for awhile."

As she opened a door and we walked into the room, Bobby's eyes lit up with recognition. It was evident from the way he looked around the room that it was identical to his own bedroom back on Earth. He willingly crawled into bed and hugged a familiar teddy bear. As I leaned over to tuck him in, he asked, "Will you leave the night light on?"

"Of course," I replied. I turned on the night light and quietly left the room. After closing the door, I asked the spirit woman, "Will he call for his mother when he wakes up?"

"No," she replied, "it is best that he forgets some things for awhile until he is ready to understand what has happened."

Then, as quickly as it had begun, my out-of-body experience was over, and I found myself back at home in my own bed. For awhile I just lay there, wondering if I had indeed been traveling astrally or if it had just been a very vivid dream.

It was not until the next morning at breakfast that I gave the incident another thought. I picked up the local newspaper and there on the front page of the *San Fernando Valley News* was the headline, "Two Children Die in Fiery Crash, Mother Badly Hurt." The words seemed to jump out at me, and I felt shaken. As I read further, I found that the accident had occurred about four miles from my home at approximately the time I lay down the day before. Two children, a little four-year-old girl and her three-year-old brother were dead at the scene of the accident. The mother had been rushed to the community hospital with second and third degree burns over sixty percent of her body. Rescue workers had difficulty freeing the woman and her two children because the car was so badly damaged.

My breakfast grew cold as I read and reread the article. It seemed to agree with everything I had experienced while traveling out-of-body. There remained one more item to check. The accident had occurred near the Van Nuys Airport underpass, and I couldn't remember seeing any grassy spot that looked like the place where the little boy and I had rested. Finally, about noon, my curiosity got the better of me and I drove over to the place where the accident had occurred. There, just as I had seen it astrally, was a newly planted strip of green grass growing in a parkway near the intersection. Although I cannot explain why I was asked to assist Bobby, I feel privileged to have been chosen to be the one to help a frightened little boy find his way to his heavenly home.

Several weeks later I communicated clairvoyantly with the spirit teacher I had met in the children's Heaven. This is her channeled message to me:

> *When an infant or child dies, whether as a result of a lingering illness or a sudden death, there stands by his side someone ready to help. Usually it is the child's own Guardian Angel. No child is left, even for a moment, without someone to comfort and care for him once he leaves the physical body.*
>
> *When babies pass over, they are taken directly to the nurseries of Heaven, where they are tended with love and care. We are every bit as concerned about the little ones that have come from Earth as any mother among you. We know that you are left with saddened hearts, but we receive each child with open arms of love. Those in charge of the babies and other children in the heavenly nurseries are specially trained. They love their work so much that no child could possibly receive better care. These infants need loving, tender care just as babies living on Earth do. So we love them, nurse them, and watch them grow into healthy, happy children.*

The children's Heaven is a protected area and parents are not allowed to enter. This is beneficial for both the children and parents. When children first arrive here, they are surrounded by forgetfulness so they are not able to remember their Earthly parents or home. Otherwise, the children would be greatly distressed because of their separation. If the parents were to visit their children, it would only cause even greater pain. When the children are emotionally ready, they are able to remember their parents and their Earthly life.

All children who die are accepted into the children's Heaven, from the newborn to those who have reached adolescence. The age varies according to mental and spiritual rather than chronological maturity. Because time in the astral world differs from time on Earth, the time each child takes to mature may vary from a few weeks to as long as twenty Earth years. Those who are more aware learn and progress at a faster rate.

I asked the spirit teacher, "If children in heaven continue to grow and mature, how will parents recognize their child when they, too, enter the World Beyond?"

When they meet on the Other Side, the child will appear just as the parents last remembered her. She will continue to look this way until that particular image is no longer needed. Then, together the parents and child can rejoice in the progress and growth that has taken place.

The children themselves choose their gradu-

ation day into the next plane of learning which corresponds to their vibrations. It is much like an Earthly graduation. Although there is eagerness to continue the great adventure, there is also reluctance to leave the children's Heaven that has provided them with so much love and security.

While I was talking about the children's Heaven, several of our group were attending a lecture in one of the classrooms at an astral university. When they joined us, they related how impressed they were with the interest that was shown for the welfare of the people of Earth. Finally all the members of our group gathered together, and we were ready to enter the celestial elevator and return to the physical world.

After returning from our astral adventure, we sat quietly for awhile. Then all the students shared their personal experiences. Many of them related how amazed they were that the middle astral looked so much like Earth. Several students had toured a laboratory where astral scientists and doctors were working on new types of medicines and methods of healing. Those who had attended the lecture were impressed with the architecture of the university buildings and the beauty of the campus with its many fountains and artistic landscaping. Melanie, whose ten-year-old sister had died of leukemia, was comforted to hear about the children's Heaven. All agreed that it had been an exciting and enlightening experience.

4

In Touch with the World Beyond

The first time I communicated with the World Beyond came as a real surprise to me. I knew that the fourth-dimensional, invisible world interpenetrates the physical world, but I didn't realize that it was possible to contact someone who had died and is now living on the Other Side. My first encounter took place more than thirty years ago.

The psychology professor was late getting to the evening class I was taking at the university. As we waited, I introduced myself to a young woman sitting next to me who appeared to be emotionally upset. She told me her name was Marge, and we chatted for awhile. Then she confessed to me that she felt as if she were on the brink of a nervous breakdown. Just then the professor arrived, and I suggested that we get together after class and finish our conversation. Later, sitting in my car in the university parking lot, she told me that her mother had died the week before after a long struggle with cancer. Without an autopsy or embalming, she was buried in the Catholic cemetery the day after her death.

That very night, her mother appeared at the foot of Marge's bed and said, "I'm not dead!" Then she disappeared. A horrible thought came to Marge: *We buried Mom and she's still alive.* Immediately Marge woke her husband and told him what she had seen and heard. His only suggestion was that she go back to sleep.

Early the next morning, Marge called the cemetery and asked that her mother's casket be exhumed. The secretary explained that she would need a permit which would take at least a week to obtain. Marge knew that by then her mother would indeed be dead, and she was overcome with frustration and grief.

After Marge had told me her story, I suggested that we get in touch with her mother. Now, it's important for you to know that I'd never talked to the dead before. In fact, the thought had never entered my mind. Yet here I was, calling out her mother's name. The first words I intuitively heard from the other side were, *Of course I'm not dead. I'm more alive than I was when I was with my daughter. Tell her I'm finally free of pain and happy to be in my new home.* As these words poured out of my mouth, a look of peace came over Marge, and she began to cry softly in relief.

After this first encounter with the astral world, I thought to myself, *If it's this easy, I'll talk to Grandma.* And so I did. When we can communicate with those who have left the Earth plane, our family and friends don't seem so far away. When someone asks me if I feel strange talking to the dead, my reply is, "They're not dead. They are more alive than we are."

Communicating with those living in the next dimension is a lot like receiving sound and pictures from a television set. First, the light and sound waves must be changed into electromagnetic waves. Then these signals are transmitted to the television receiver. Finally, the receiver unscrambles the signals and changes them back into light and sound waves. Television cannot send a picture of an entire scene all at once. It sends one part at a time until it has sent the complete picture. The electronic signals are fed into the TV set's tuner. The tuner selects only the channel the viewer wants to receive and shuts out all others.

Just as light and sound waves travel through the air, thought waves can travel from one person to another. The brain of the transmitter sends out vibrations, and the brain of the receiver registers the thought waves by means of the pineal gland. When a message is sent from someone in the astral world, her thoughts produce electromagnetic waves which are transmitted to a physical person. It is fitting that we call this person a "channel" because she is able, with the help of her Higher Self, to tune into these particular thoughts and shut out all others. Only a part of the message is given at a time. When these words have been spoken or written, then the next part of the message is sent.

When we are making contact with the Other Side, we need to surround ourselves mentally with the White Light of protection. Anyone who is gullible or careless can be completely deceived by astral inhabitants from the lower levels who enjoy playing tricks on Earth people. When a message comes from the astral world, it should be treated in the same way we would consider a suggestion from someone in the physical world. We need to use our own judgment to determine whether the information is valid or not. Remember that all communication coming from the World Beyond is filtered through the mind of both the sender and receiver. So, consciously or unconsciously, the communication may be colored with their own thoughts and feelings.

When a friend or family member steps through the door of death, they do not become all-knowing and all wise. In fact, they will have the same mentality and personality that they had when they were living on Earth. So when we put questions to them, we should not expect an answer beyond their own intelligence. Grandpa won't know the winning lottery number for next week, and your aunt can't tell you when the next earthquake will occur. That does not mean that they will not grow in wisdom, for there are countless halls of learning and universities in the astral world where they may study and increase their knowledge and understanding.

From the earliest times, people have been interested in getting in touch with the Other Side. Many races and religions believed that the gods took a personal interest in human affairs and that their priests and priestesses were able to channel the messages of the gods to the people. In the land of Israel, it was the prophets who claimed to be directly in touch with God. It was the prophet's responsibility to channel God's message to the people. The ancient Greeks and Romans believed that the gods spoke to them through oracles; then a priest or priestess would interpret the meaning of the message.

In ancient Rome there were also male channelers, called "soothsayers" or "augurs." They believed that the gods revealed their wishes through certain signs or omens, such as thunder and lightning or the flight of birds. There was even a college where the augurs learned their craft. Sibyls were the female channelers of their day. After purifying herself, the sibyl would inhale the smoke of laurel leaves, which helped her to enter a trance state. She would then give her message to those who had gathered to hear her words of wisdom.

Channeling is an effective way of making contact with the next dimension. To channel, it is necessary to achieve an altered state of consciousness. Because there are varying degrees in the alpha state, we need to find the one that we are most comfortable with in order to channel. It's difficult to explain the differences in the depths of the astral state. In a way, we can relate it to the process we experience each night as we fall asleep. When we first lie down, we begin to unwind from the stress of the day. Then as we relax and close our eyes, our breathing and heartbeat begin to slow down and our mind becomes quiet. Finally, we are no longer aware of our surroundings and we are asleep. The more we practice, the easier it becomes to choose the depth of our altered state of consciousness.

In the light alpha state, we are conscious of what is being channeled through us. The problem is that the left brain (analytic mind) may try to influence the message. In a slightly deeper alpha state, we are still able to hear our channeled words and use this information to increase our awareness and spiritual growth, but the experience is like trying to remember our dreams, which often fade away. Deeper yet in the alpha state, we may have a vague sense of the message but remember only bits and pieces. Some feel that real channeling occurs only in the deepest alpha or trance state. They are no longer aware of the words that they are speaking or of what is going on around them. They may even be out of their physical body and traveling astrally.

Spontaneous channeling may occur more often than we realize. We may be speaking to someone on the phone or in person, and out of our mouth come words of wisdom that are just what that person needed to hear. Perhaps we are writing a letter or article and we find ourselves amazed at the beauty and poetry of the words we have put down on paper.

Whether we are speaking to just one person or to a room full of people, conscious channeling is more like a lecture being given from the World Beyond. So it's important that we overcome any sense of self-consciousness or stage fright and let the pure message come through. We need to put aside our ego and let the words from the Other Side channel through us.

Many people in the last ten or fifteen years have stepped forward to bring us channeled information from the Masters. Perhaps it is best that I do not list the current channelers, lest I omit someone's name.

If a person charges an unreasonably large amount of money to hear the channeled words of a Master, look at the purity of his motives. If someone gives the impression that he is as important as the Master who channels through him, be careful — he may be on an ego trip. If someone says that a certain Master will channel only through him, then the Master is probably his own Higher Self.

It is important to remember that the message that comes through those who channel is not only colored by their individual belief systems, but those who dwell in the higher astral realms also have their own perspectives and philosophies. Thus, information transmitted from the astral world usually contains personal opinions, judgments, or predictions that may or may not be accurate. Therefore, discernment is needed in judging the validity of all channeled messages.

When we receive a channeled message, we can repeat it aloud or we can write it down. I have found that one of the most valuable methods of getting in touch with the World Beyond is through inspirational writing. Some people confuse inspirational writing with automatic writing. Edgar Cayce, Ruth Montgomery, and others warn against automatic writing because it is a type of possession. In automatic writing, an astral citizen takes over and moves the physical writer's hand and arm. The one sending the message could be from the lower astral planes and might try to trick you into believing an untruth. The message may even be in a foreign language, or mirror writing. In inspirational writing, by contrast, the ideas come from the Other Side but your own handwriting and spelling errors appear in the channeled message.

When you are ready to do inspirational writing, quiet yourself, go into the alpha state, and circle yourself with White Light. Then write down a question addressed to your Higher Self, to another of the Masters, or to friends or family who are on the Other Side. Write down the first word or two that comes into your mind. Sometimes no more of the message will be sent until they know you have received the first few words.

If you have difficulty learning to write intuitively, try using your left hand, even though the writing may not be very legible. The reason this method may work is that we are cross-wired. The right side of the brain (creative and intuitive) controls the left side of the body, including the left hand.

The typewriter and computer are excellent tools in helping us make contact with the Other Side, especially if you can type with your eyes closed. This allows you to go deeper into the alpha state, which may help you receive a more accurate message that is not colored by your own beliefs and opinions. Typing is a much faster way of receiving inspirational writing. Once you get started, the words will often rush into your mind faster and faster.

When we learn to do inspirational writing, it makes it possible to keep in touch with family and friends who have entered the World Beyond. I had been a close friend of Bob and his family during my high school days. When I heard that Bob had been killed in an airplane crash, I contacted him in the spirit world because I was interested in learning from Bob himself what had happened. This is the message that he relayed to me through inspirational writing:

> *It had started out as one of those beautiful California days that make you feel that life is truly worth living. A friend and I drove out to the airport where I kept my small plane. It was a perfect day for flying. As the engine warmed up, we were discussing whether we should fly south over the San Fernando Valley or west and circle over the Pacific Ocean.*
>
> *The plane lifted off the ground and began to gain altitude when something went wrong. The plane barely cleared the water tower, and a split second later it lay crumpled against the hillside. I found myself sitting on the ground outside the plane. As I stood up, I said to myself how lucky I was that I wasn't hurt. I went over to help pull Ray out of the plane. As I did this, I looked over and there on the front seat was me. Boy! Did that throw me for a loop. I really was at a loss to explain it. It took some time and a lot of patient explanation by a couple of spirit helpers to convince me that I was no longer living in my old body but in a new one of the spirit. I guess the feeling I had would be described as confused and stunned. I felt no physical change. I felt as good in my new body as I had in the body that I saw the medics take away in the ambulance.*
>
> *I think that when death is unexpected it makes it that much harder. A spirit guide explained to me that sudden death allows no time for preparation. One second you are in your*

physical body, the next you are not. At first, you may not realize that you are dead because your new body appears to be similar to the physical one you just left. You will have no pain although you may not realize this at first. You may even try to finish doing something you were about to do and were unable to complete. You may try to speak to someone or touch them, but they will probably pay no attention to you. By this time, you may be so frustrated you decide you are having a terrifying nightmare.

I personally did not know what to expect at death, and I found it very hard at first to even believe that I had died because I felt so very much alive. I looked around for awhile because I did not want to leave. I wanted to be sure that Ray was taken care of, and I was trying to figure out what had gone wrong with the plane. The spirit people were patient for a long while and waited on the sidelines, but finally, they quietly insisted that we must be going. When I got to Heaven, Mom and Dad were there to welcome me. I really felt like I had come home.

When you do inspirational writing it will sometimes be prose, sometimes poetry, sometimes just seemingly disconnected words. If you wish to keep a spiritual diary, arrange a special time each day to make contact with your Higher Self. It's a good idea to date each message for future reference. Stored in the memory bank of your Higher Self is the knowledge you have gained in all your past lives. If additional wisdom is sought, your Higher Self has access to unlimited cosmic knowledge. What a treasure trove of information is available simply for the asking!

Many have found that learning to channel has changed their lives for the better. Channeling can be a major step toward enlightenment. It enables us to receive guidance, inspiration, and wisdom from the Masters, including our Higher Self.

Some people might think that when they make contact with the World Beyond, a wise Being will tell them what to do and solve all their problems for them. Instead, they find that they still need to make their own decisions and work out their own problems. It's important to understand that the Masters, including our Higher Self, will give advice to help us but will not take away from us our free will or interfere with the lessons we have chosen to learn that will enable us to grow and evolve. With the Master's help, we can see the whole picture more clearly so that we can take the appropriate actions and accomplish our chosen tasks with greater wisdom.

There are other ways besides channeling to get in touch with people in the next dimension. The crystal ball has been used for many centuries as a means of obtaining information from the astral world. Small spheres of crystal were found in tombs of the ancient Franks that date back more than two thousand years. The Incas used small crystalline objects for divining. By gazing into a crystal ball for a period of time, one can reach a semi-trance or alpha state. Then a field of energy will appear to swirl inside the crystal ball, and gradually a picture will begin to form which helps give an answer to a question. The problem I have experienced is that reflected light is also visible in the crystal ball. As yet, I haven't figured out how to overcome this problem.

Some people use rune tiles to receive a message from the astral world. The term *rune* comes from the Old Norse word meaning "secret." The Norsemen believed that their chief god, Odin, invented the runic characters. Each tile has a character on it that conveys a special meaning. Ancient priests used the runes to foretell the future. I keep my runes in a special bag from which I draw seven tiles. Interpreting these rune tiles can help answer a question that has been asked.

For centuries, tea leaves have been used as a point of concentration as we tune into the Other Side. When I was a teenager, I would give readings to members of my family using tea leaves. In those days tea came in bulk, so there were always stray leaves in each cup. The person who wanted a reading left a little tea and the leaves in the bottom of the cup. I would carefully turn the cup upside down on the saucer and turn the cup around three times clockwise. Then I would quiet myself and stare at the leaves, which seemed to form pictures that gave answers to the questions.

Tarot is one of my favorite methods of contacting the Other Side. People ask me how they can learn to read the cards and my answer is, "Take time to get to know each card. Enter the alpha state and become a part of the card. Take note of all the details. Jot down what the card means to you. Then compare your ideas with the information that came with your deck. Write down several key words that will remind you of the meaning of this card. When you are giving a reading, you may want to start with the key words for that card and then tune in to your Higher Self for the message from the Other Side. You will probably find that it is easier to give someone else a reading than to do one for yourself."

The Ouija board is another way of contacting the next dimension. On the board are printed letters of the alphabet, numbers from 0 to 9, plus *yes* and *no* (*oui* is

French for "yes"; *ja* is German for "yes"). Two people put their fingers lightly on the pointer, which spells out answers to questions. My Higher Self advises me not to use the Ouija board because, usually, only the lower astral citizens communicate in this manner. Be especially careful if you do choose to use an Ouija board, since you could unknowingly attract a negative astral person who might decide to hang around for awhile and cause trouble.

People are discovering that the pendulum is a good way of getting answers from the World Beyond. The pendulum can consist of a gold or silver chain, or even a string, with a weight on the end. Ideally, the weight should be a crystal or special talisman. The pendulum needs to be "trained." Hold the chain at the end so the pendulum can swing freely. Tell it that swinging along one axis means "yes"; swinging on the other axis means "no"; and swinging in a circle means "maybe." Your training chart should look like a plus sign surrounded by a circle. Once the pendulum has been trained, you can ask your Higher Self questions, and the answers will be given through the swinging pendulum.

Whatever way we choose to make contact with the World Beyond, the process is much the same. It is necessary to achieve an altered state of consciousness by making the physical body as relaxed and comfortable as possible and by quieting the mind. Then we need to tune into the message being sent by our Higher Self. As we practice, we will find that it becomes easier and easier to be in touch with the World Beyond.

Perhaps you are one of the thousands of people who have heard audible astral voices at some time in your life. Often it's a word of caution or a voice calling a name. Virginia Seeley heard an unexpected voice that prevented a serious accident. Here is her story:

"Many years ago, I was working the night shift at a lunch counter in a drugstore. This particular night we closed at midnight as usual. It was cold so I had all the windows of my car rolled up as I drove home along Vermont Avenue. The signal was green as I approached Exposition Boulevard, but suddenly a man's deep voice commanded me to stop! I immediately slammed on my brakes and skidded to a stop. Out of nowhere, a car crossed in front of me as it ran the red light. My car rocked from side to side as the other automobile sped past me.

"A couple of people standing on the corner waiting for a bus were absolutely petrified. They had seen the other car speeding toward the intersection and thought that the two cars would collide. They couldn't understand how I had stopped so suddenly. A man ran over to my car and asked if I was all right. 'I think so,' I replied shakily.

"'I'm so thankful you stopped,' continued the man. 'We knew you couldn't see the speeding car, and we were sure you would be hit. What made you stop so suddenly?'

"'Someone in my car told me to stop,' I responded weakly. The man gave me a funny look, and together we checked the back seat of my car, but there was no one there. As I drove the rest of the way home, I began to realize that the one who commanded me to stop and had saved me from a serious accident, possibly even death, was my guardian angel sent to protect me from harm."

The audible voice phenomenon has attracted the interest of electronic engineers as well as clergymen and parapsychologists. Hundreds of scientific researchers and even a larger number of amateur investigators have successfully carried out experiments. They have taped voices they believe have come from friends and relatives on the Other Side. As scientists continue to explore the link between the physical and astral world, they are experimenting with a number of different recording techniques. When the voices from the next dimension are recorded, they are usually faint and rapid with an unusual rhythm, pitch, or intensity. When we consider the difficulties involved in lowering their vibrations to our Earthly level, it is amazing that we are able to obtain any kind of success in producing an actual recording of astral voices.

Dreams are another way of getting in touch with the World Beyond. There are several different types of dreams. Some are of little or no value to us because they usually pertain to something we've been involved in during that day. Other dreams are really not dreams at all but out-of-body experiences. There is another type of dream that puts us in direct contact with the Other Side. If we pay attention to these dreams, it is like having a personal counselor to help us cope with our problems. This counselor is a genius, pointing out aspects of our situation that we may have overlooked or ignored. Of course, this counselor is our own Guardian Angel or Higher Self.

I tell my students, "To remember and learn from your dreams, you need to record them as soon as possible. It's wise to keep a paper and pencil by your bed. Write down, in story form, as much as you can remember. Let the story speak to you for a few hours before you begin to analyze the dream. Dreams are rich in symbolism and imagery. For this reason, they may be difficult to interpret. It may require a good deal of effort and practice to decode a dream. Because a dream is a highly personal experience, you alone are able to fully appreciate and interpret its meaning. A dream can give you help in solving a problem or warn against a plan of action. Dreams can be a bridge between you and your Higher Self."

There are times when a warning received through a dream has been heeded and impending disaster avoided. One night, a mother dreamed that she was standing in her daughter's room when an earthquake loosened a heavy light fixture, causing it to fall onto the bed and kill her child. The mother woke her husband and told him her terrifying dream. He said it was a silly dream and told her to go back to sleep. The dream did appear to be ridiculous, but the mother couldn't get back to sleep. She finally got up and brought the child back to her own bed. Several hours later, just as in her dream, an earthquake caused the heavy light fixture to fall onto the bed right where the child's head would have been. By heeding the warning given in the dream, the mother saved her daughter's life.

Probably the easiest and most direct way to get in touch with the World Beyond is through meditation. We all need to find our own unique ways of meditating. Some people enjoy meditating in a group, while others prefer to be alone. Some people sit cross-legged on the floor, while others are more comfortable sitting on a chair or even ly-ing down. Some people focus on a particular object, such as a candle flame or a flower petal. Still others just let thoughts and ideas flow through their minds. For some, five minutes is long enough, while others spend at least half an hour in meditation. Personally, I am more interested in the depth of the experience than in the length of time spent in meditation.

To meditate, we need to relax, close our eyes, become quiet, enter the alpha state, and listen within our hearts to the message of our Higher Self. There will always be distractions: a dog barks; a car goes by. This is a natural part of living. But we need to prepare as quiet an environment as possible so that we are not disturbed during our time of meditation.

One of our supreme attainments in the physical world is to communicate consciously with our beloved Higher Self through prayer and meditation. Prayer is our conversation with our personal God — our Higher Self. We can talk as we would to a good friend, petitioning, praising, and giving thanks. Then we need to be still and listen. In meditation, we quiet the conscious mind and tune into our Higher Self.

Above the astral world, in the higher dimensions, dwell Archangels, our Higher Self, and Ascended Masters (those who have successfully completed their lives on Earth). As we raise our consciousness to a higher level, our inspiration and wisdom will come from these great Masters who embody pure love and cosmic wisdom. The information that is channeled to us from these great Beings is Universal Truth.

5

The Enchanting World of Nature Spirits

It was an extremely hot evening, and the students and I were grateful for the air-conditioned coolness of the classroom. When the students had settled in their seats, I told them, "Tonight we are going to astrally visit an enchanting glen in the middle planes of the World Beyond. Now quiet yourselves, get comfortable, relax, and prepare to enter the astral elevator that will take us to tonight's adventure."

When we stepped off the astral elevator, we found ourselves in the middle of a meadow of wild flowers. A great variety of nature spirits live in this glen. The students and I enjoyed watching the fairies flitting gracefully from flower to flower, while the zephyrs floated above us, creating a gentle breeze. A brook flowed through the meadow into a tranquil pool, where some water sprites splashed in play. As my students became better acquainted with these etheric beings, they began to understand how dependent we are on the nature spirits who reside in the astral world.

There are a great variety of etheric beings, both large and small, who live and work in the unseen world around us. They work in cooperation with nature by stimulating the growth of plants and trees, by influencing the winds and the rain, and by guiding the instincts of animals. Their order of evolution runs parallel to our own. As they evolve, their mentality and sense of responsibility increase accordingly. Therefore, a fairy does not remain a fairy forever but progresses in the course of eons into an angel of the Air Kingdom.

Angels and nature spirits have no fixed, solid bodies as we understand the term. Their astral bodies are extremely fluid, and they are able to change their size and appearance at will. Their bodies are iridescent and pulsating with astral forces that are not limited to a fixed or definite shape. Sometimes they appear to be globes of light. The energy that radiates from this center builds up wings and filmy shapes of vaguely human semblance. Because they are asexual, they might materialize in either a female or male form to carry out their assigned tasks.

Common tradition has always recognized the existence of fairies, elves, gnomes, and other nature spirits, and they seem to enjoy having a ready-made thought form in which to appear. Clairvoyants have observed them looking very much like their traditional storybook image.

There are many different kinds of etheric beings, and sometimes areas that are close together are inhabited by different kinds of nature spirit. Despite their differences, they have much in common, sometimes appearing friendly and sometimes mischievous or even unfriendly. Most of these nature spirits seem to respond to human emotion and appear to appreciate kindly attention and affection.

In olden days, nature spirits were more easily observed than they are today. Leprechauns could be seen running across the green fields of Ireland and playing pranks on Irish farmers. Tradition says that in ancient Hawaii, the menehunes sometimes helped the natives by building, in one night, rock walls across the openings of small inlets. The Hawaiians used these sheltered pools as fish ponds, some of which can still be seen on the islands today.

In Switzerland, the little hill-men were kind and friendly. Folklore relates that they would sometimes drive home stray lambs and even supply peasants with firewood. In the past, they could be seen swarming over the hills, but in modern times they seem to prefer to remain invisible. Scandinavian people had their mischievous trolls, who were grotesque in appearance and considered good for nothing. The manikins of Germany were believed to dwell in underground caverns lined with gold. These caves had no entrances because manikins, like all nature spirits, can pass through solid things, such as rocks and earth, just as easily as through the air. They would often reward those who pleased them but play pranks on any who offended them.

The legends of Persia tell of two kinds of beings, the deeves and the peris. The peris were friendly toward humans, and the female peris were especially beautiful. The deeves, on the other hand, were unfriendly, and both the male and female were grotesquely ugly. Nordic people believed in elves. Some of the elves lived in underground caves and were ugly and misshapen. Other elves were well formed and symmetrical. They flew on gauzy wings and danced in the meadows. If left undisturbed, they would delight in doing kind deeds for humans, but if interfered with, they retaliated with mischief.

Children seem to be able to see fairies and other nature spirits more readily than adults. This may be true because children are more open-minded or because these etheric beings do not fear them as much as they do adults. Seeing fairies is often a once-in-a-lifetime experience.

My friend Ruth tells of her chance encounter with the enchanting world of fairies:

> *"When I was about four and a half years old, I awakened from my afternoon nap and glanced out of my bedroom window. I was amazed to see that a tree near our house was filled with little people about five or six inches tall. The females were wearing long dresses with the skirts gathered at the waist. They had long sleeves and large, white ruffled collars. They wore white aprons tied at the waist that hung down over their dresses. On their heads they wore white caps with ruffles all around. The males wore long, black jackets that went nearly to their knees and buttoned up the front. Their pants came to just below their knees, and many of them were wearing black hats with tall crowns and wide brims.*
>
> *"These little beings were playing all over the branches of the tree. Some were swinging, some jumping rope, and others sitting at round tables sipping from tiny cups. I lay there taking it all in until my eyes grew tired from staring. When I blinked my eyes, all the little fairies had disappeared from my sight. Later when I told my family about my experience, they thought I was just pretending, but I know what I saw. I know I had a brief glimpse into the fairy world."*

On the rare occasions when nature spirits have been observed physically, it has usually been on a very hot, still day, conditions that help to raise the surrounding vibrations to a higher frequency level. So when the day is warm and there is no wind, you may notice one little blade of grass moving back and forth. Look closely, for it could be a nature spirit enjoying the beauty of a new day. Nora tells of just such an encounter:

> *"All of nature seemed to be sleeping as I strolled along a country road near my home. Not a leaf was moving that hot summer afternoon. Suddenly my attention was drawn to a single, blade-like leaf of an iris. While the rest of the plant was motionless, this one leaf was moving rapidly up and down. Expecting to find a grasshopper or some small rodent, I stepped quietly up to the plant.*
>
> *"There, to my utter astonishment, was a tiny, green nature spirit swinging happily back and forth on the leaf. His tiny feet were crossed over the blade, while his hands held onto the leaf above his head. This merry little nature spirit appeared to be about four inches tall. For a minute or so, he remained in view, swinging on the leaf. Then he vanished from my sight. Many times since that special day, I have seen a single leaf moving violently while the rest of the plant remained motionless, but I have never again been able to see the cause of the movement."*

Sir Arthur Conan Doyle, creator of Sherlock Holmes, wrote a delightful book entitled *The Coming of the Fairies.* In his book are pictures taken by two young English girls, Frances and Elsie, reportedly showing fairies in all their delicate beauty. One photograph taken by Elsie on a bright, sunny day in July 1917 shows Frances and a group of fairies with a waterfall and rocks in the background. The original negative was inspected by expert photographers and showed no double exposure or retouching. It appeared to be a single-exposure picture, although it was somewhat overexposed. Later, in August 1920, Elsie was given a negative from a packet in which each plate had been secretly marked. After Elsie took a picture of her friend, Frances, with a fairy, the negative was carefully examined. There was no trace of its being anything other than a genuine photograph.

Are these, indeed, real pictures of nature spirits? It would be necessary for the fairies to slow down their vibrations before they could be photographed. To my knowledge, these are the only photographs of nature spirits in existence. The debate is still going on: are these pictures real or not?

Nature spirits differ from us in that they do not have free will or ego. Therefore, they are able to concentrate all their energies on their work. The tiny entities have only a mass consciousness. Fairies, brownies, and elves seem to work at their tasks like bees in a hive without any individual responsibility. The more evolved nature spirits and angels attain a higher level of consciousness. The higher angels know nature's plan, and by telepathy they make it known to the ranks below them. Each group has its leader who in turn is responsible to a more advanced group. At the top of their hierarchical system are the great Archangels.

Fairies, the infants of the Air Kingdom, are minute in both size and development. Fairies do not seem to understand what they do or why but are led by instinct. They have been clairvoyantly seen flitting through the air in short flights, pausing a moment between each flight to touch the flower or leaf where they have come to rest.

If you want to create a sanctuary for the fairies and

nature spirits in your yard, provide an attractive place with flowers, plants, rocks, and perhaps a fountain or pond. As often as possible, spend quiet time in this sanctuary, sending out thoughts of love. As the nature spirits become familiar with your presence, they may make themselves known to you.

It takes time, patience, and a simple, childlike faith to become aware of the nature spirits. As you water your indoor plants, perhaps you can find time to talk to them. (By the way, most plants prefer tepid water and they love to be misted.) As the nature spirits feel your vibrations of love surrounding them and begin to trust you, they will become braver, until at last they may make themselves known to you. People with green thumbs are really those who have learned to communicate telepathically with the nature spirits dwelling within the plant's form. As the plant spirits awaken to your desire to communicate, you will notice an increase in energy each time you come close to them. Then you can listen intuitively to the message coming from a plant's indwelling spirit. My friend Margot Nation tells this delightful story about her experience with nature spirits:

> *"At one time, I had about fifty plants in my home, most of which I had arranged on shelves in my kitchen where they could catch the morning sun. Because of the varied species, I had to make daily rounds to check their individual watering needs.*
>
> *"One morning while going through my usual ritual of greeting and complimenting them on their beauty, I noticed a strange glow around two of the larger plants. Thinking that my eyes were deceiving me, I looked closer and was about to*

touch them when the glow changed into multicolored balls of light. I was absolutely stunned! The balls of light were bobbing up and down on the leaves and seemed to react to my feelings of curiosity and excitement. Then they abruptly disappeared. I continued to watch the plants intently for a long while but saw nothing more that was out of the ordinary.

"Several days passed and I had nearly forgotten the incident when our family cat came rushing up to the plants. She stood on her hind legs and looked as if she were about to leap up on the shelf. As I picked my cat up, I realized what had attracted her attention, for there was a glow like the one I had observed before. As I watched, the glow changed into balls of pink, blue, green, yellow, and lavender. They seemed to dance from leaf to leaf to a melody beyond the range of my hearing. Suddenly, new forms took shape before my eyes. These shapes looked almost human — like enchanting little females with large eyes. They seemed very much aware of my presence, and they smiled up at me. They were about two inches high. Some were blond, while others had long dark hair.

"After that, my little plant fairies appeared quite often, usually at my request. They seemed to enjoy the attention I gave them. Occasionally, they tried to entice my cat, only to find themselves and their plant homes knocked to the floor. Plant fairies, I discovered, seem to increase their beauty and willingness to take form when they sense a true reverence toward nature."

The nature spirits who dwell within the plants respond to both negative and positive emotions. They are also affected by the sounds around them. They seem to prefer soft, soothing music. Working with nature spirits is an ongoing process of communicating and sharing with nature.

Fairies, like all nature spirits, meet many deaths or changes of form. Whenever their work is completed, the old body is left behind and another, more lovely in color and form, is prepared for them. After experiencing many of these body changes, a fairy eventually evolves into a zephyr.

The baby zephyr emerges less than a foot tall but will attain a stature of about three feet. Zephyrs possess a rare beauty. Their bodies sometimes appear to be a shimmering sapphire color, while at other times they appear in various shades of yellow. The young learn to glide upon waves of air; the older zephyrs control the air currents of Earth. Zephyrs often move about us in gentle or playful breezes.

Next are the sylphs, who are wiser and more developed than the fairies or zephyrs. The sylphs grow to be three to five feet in height. Although they are not yet angels, they possess a high degree of mentality and are far more intuitive than most humans. Sylphs work with etheric conditions created by solar and cosmic forces. Although sylphs are asexual, as are all those evolving to angelhood, they appear in female form with faces that are strangely beautiful. They appear to have white wings attached to their bodies at the shoulders and reaching down to their feet; however, this is an illusion produced by the astral energy flowing through their auras.

Above the sylphs are those who have reached angelhood. The Angels of the Wind are in charge of all the air currents which are caused by the rotation of the Earth. The Angels of Force are in charge of storms and other turbulent conditions, while the Angels of Calm control the elements that induce fair, sunny weather. The highest and most developed angels of the Air Kingdom are the Archangels. They are in charge of all decisions regarding climate changes and rainfall.

People's negative actions, thoughts, and emotions build up destructive energies in the air. When this negativity grows to a dangerous level, it is imperative that the power be released. To keep the whole planet from being affected by this negative energy, the Archangels permit areas to be cleansed. When a natural catastrophe occurs, it is nature's way of dispersing the destructive energy that has accumulated in the atmosphere. Hurricanes, typhoons, tornadoes, and lightning storms are some of the ways Angels of Force disperse these negative energies.

During severe storms, the younger angels are sent out of the disturbed areas, while only the advanced angels remain to keep vigil at a safe distance. When the Angels of Force have completed their work and the storm has abated, the angels return and once again take up their work with the air currents, evaporation, changes in weather, and the rhythm of the seasons.

Frankins are one group of etheric beings who work with the Plant and Mineral kingdoms. These are beautiful, little creatures of childlike appearance. They live in their etheric bodies a very long time before realizing death. They then move forward to their next step of evolvement. In the etheric realm, work is not accomplished with hands: the youngest perform their work through rhythms of breath, while the more advanced angels use their creative intelligence.

Elves also belong to the Plant and Mineral kingdoms. They do not appear to be clothed but are covered with a tight-fitting brown skin which shines as if wet and is surrounded by a small, green aura. Their legs are thin and their hands and feet seem large and out of proportion to the rest of their bodies. Elves' ears and noses are pointed and their mouths are wide and toothless. They grow to be fifteen to twenty-four inches tall. Elves care for growing things such as plants and small shrubs.

Next are the gnomes, who some believe are a relic of ancient Atlantis. They can reach a height of thirty inches and are usually lanky and grotesque in appearance. Their arms seem too long for their bodies and, like their legs, are bent at the joints as if they had grown stiff with age. In fact, their whole appearance and bearing gives the impression of extreme old age. The gnomes' eyes are small and black, and their complexion is rough and coarse. Gnomes live for a very long time, but the passage of time appears to make little or no impression upon them either mentally or physically. Their movements are quaint and stiff but, like all etheric creatures, they can move below the surface of the ground without any effort. Gnomes seem to develop a kind of affection for the tree roots, rocks, and earth which make up and surround their home.

Yosemite, with its many nature spirits, has always been a very special place to me. One day I found a rather secluded spot beside a rushing river. As I sat quietly eating my picnic lunch, I sensed a gnome emerging from the roots of a nearby pine tree. This nature spirit seemed shy and quickly retreated when startled by a sudden noise. Finally the gnome became braver, and we were able to communicate mentally for some time before he again slipped back into his underground home.

Gnomes are generally solitary, but sometimes a gnome may become interested in a human being. Folklore relates that a gnome may even tell a human where a treasure lies. This treasure may be a simple rock, or it could be a mineral deposit of great worth. Their consciousness is primitive and limited, but they appear to get great joy from imitating human behavior.

Brownies, like gnomes, are generally found on or just beneath the surface of the ground and among the roots of trees and plants. Brownies appear to be of medieval origin because their attire resembles that of countrymen of that period: a short brown coat with bright buttons, brown knee breeches, rough stockings, boots, and a long, pointed cap. A brownie's weatherbeaten face and gray beard give the impression of old age. Their eyes are small and beady, but they have a kindly, simple expression. By nature, they are friendly and often live in tribes. Their height varies from four to twelve inches.

More advanced in the Plant and Mineral kingdoms are the tree devas who, in height and size, resemble the tree that is in their care. The older tree devas strengthen the etheric body of the tallest and oldest trees in the immediate vicinity, while less developed tree spirits work with younger trees. Many of the younger tree spirits appear to have long, dark, somewhat tangled hair which gives them a rather wild look. They may not seem beautiful by our standards because their features are elongated and narrow. Their shape from the waist down is seldom clearly defined. A tree deva may take on some of the appearance of the species of tree in its care. For example, part of the aura of a pine tree deva resembles clothing with fringes that look like hanging pine needles.

In my back yard I have a grove of evergreen trees. Several years ago, I noticed that the needles of one of the larger pines had turned brown and were falling off. Soon the whole tree was dead and had to be cut down. As I was raking up the dried pine needles, I thought to myself, *Why did that beautiful pine die while all the rest look so healthy?*

In answer, I heard a voice inside my head reply, *Do you not see that it was necessary for one to die so the smaller trees might receive the sunlight they need to grow strong and healthy?* I immediately saw the truth in this and realized that one tree had sacrificed itself so that the surrounding trees might have life.

Tree devas seem unaffected by the passage of time, as if our seasons were but days to them. Their consciousness is not focused upon the physical plane, although they are aware of the existence of humans. If you feel the need for an energy boost or you need comforting, hug a tree or lean against it. As you touch the trunk, the energy of the deva will begin to flow through the tree to you. If possible, develop a relationship with a particular tree and it will become easier and easier to interact with that tree deva.

Every mountain has its own angelic guardian, who is called the "Spirit of the Mountain." The size of these angels varies from an average height of ten feet to thirty feet or more. Above them are the Archangels who supervise all those who work in or near the mountain range in their care.

Oceanids, the smallest etheric forms of the Water Kingdom, are no larger than a drop of water. Through evaporation, these oceanids are lifted into the air and then deposited as rain where they are needed. Oceanids eventually evolve into water sprites, which are about eight inches in height. They are still not aware of any individual purpose, but they ride the waters gleefully as they travel to the sea.

Sea nymphs are the next stage of evolvement and are from one and a half to two feet in height; they have female bodies that are radiantly beautiful. They live in colonies under or on the surface of the sea. Their reason for existence seems to be joyously riding on the waves.

As I was returning home from Catalina Island one summer on the *Great White Steamship*, I found a few minutes to be alone. While I was standing on the lower deck gazing out over the beautiful Pacific, I clairvoyantly saw and heard a group of sea nymphs shrieking joyously to each other as they raced along beside our boat. What a pleasure it was to see such carefree happiness!

On the next step up are the naiads, who are at least a foot taller than the sea nymphs. Naiads prefer fresh water. Their experience and intelligence are greater, and they understand the importance of the duties they perform and know that the will of the River King must be obeyed. They also realize that each river has a destiny and a purpose.

The nature spirits who belong to the Water Kingdom are much more keenly alive and active than those who serve on land. Another characteristic is the rapidity with which they change their form. Many appear to spend all their time skimming swiftly over the surface of the water, now diving, now shooting high into the air in a state of exultant joy. There is a strong sense of rivalry, so there is much friction, instability, and excitability among those who are below the grade of angel. This rivalry exists between the nature spirits in different rivers as well as those in adjoining oceans.

The River King is in charge of all flowing water, while the seas and oceans are ruled over by powerful Archangels. The supreme leader of all the water beings is an Archangel of high rank who, with his aides, decides the destinies of the mingling of water and wind in order to bring about changes in climate whenever and wherever these changes are needed.

Besides the nature spirits and angels who are concerned with the Air, Water, Plant and Mineral kingdoms, there are those who care for the welfare of animals. When we accept the responsibility of a pet, it is important that we take care not only of its physical but also of its emotional needs. We can communicate either aloud or mentally with our pet. In turn, our pet communicates with body language and intuitively, as well as with a bark or meow. It is not only important that we treat our pets with love and kindness; we also need to teach them obedience and constructive behavior.

The angels who care for the physical welfare of animals do so by telepathy. Through thought waves, an angel can guide the animal's instincts toward finding food and shelter, providing for its offspring, and caring for itself when ill or in danger. When it is time for salmon to spawn, an angel guides them upstream — sometimes as far as two thousand miles from the ocean — to the place where they were hatched. Angels guide birds as they migrate. Each fall bobolinks fly four to five thousand miles south, and each spring they fly back again through the uncharted airways.

Younger angels have fewer animals in their care; more advanced angels have a wider field of service. Young angels regulate the instincts of the very small and relatively unevolved animals such as insects and rodents. These animals live only a short time, for it is important that they experience rapid births and deaths so that they may e-volve. Some insects live only a few days, but death is a much simpler process for animals than it is for humans. At death, the animal spirit returns to the Group Soul, and at birth it comes back in a body that is one step higher in consciousness.

When animals incarnate, they remain in the same species. For example, canines incarnate over thousands of lifetimes from jackals, coyotes, foxes, wolves, and finally to domesticated dogs.

Angels watch for animals who have experienced love and in turn are able to show love and have also developed their individual traits and characteristics. From then on, the animal spirit will no longer return to the Group Soul at death, but it will be kept individually. Thus, it is possible for the spirit of a beloved pet to return to the same master in another body at another time.

When we returned from our astral tour of the world of nature spirits, the students shared their experiences and expressed their amazement at the variety of nature spirits that they had observed. Florence said, "Until tonight I hadn't even been aware of the existence and activities of these etheric beings. I'm amazed at how they cooperate with nature in stimulating the growth of plants and trees, influencing the winds and the rain, and guiding the instincts of the animals in their care."

Robert told the class, "Now I have a better understanding of the interdependence that exists between ourselves and the nature spirits, from the smallest fairy to the greatest Archangel."

6

A Variety of Ghosts

It may surprise you to learn that when we are traveling astrally we may be mistakenly identified as ghosts. Our astral body can easily go through physical objects such as a wall, a roof, or even a human being. If we should happen to walk through a physical person, he may experience a strange, cold feeling which might convince him that he has just had an encounter with a ghost.

The term "apparition," which means an unusual or unexpected sight, is more appropriate than the word "ghost" when we are referring to someone who is alive and traveling astrally. Besides people who are consciously traveling astrally, some apparitions may be people who have experienced a spontaneous astral projection because of an overdose of drugs or alcohol, or during some life crisis such as an accident, illness, or near-death experience. Some may be deeply asleep or unconscious while their astral bodies are out exploring. When apparitions appear to friends or relatives, they can often be recognized.

Ghosts are probably the most misunderstood and frightening inhabitants of the World Beyond as they interact with us in the physical world. The unseen world is peopled by a variety of ghosts who come in all types and sizes. Some are friendly, some mischievous, and still others just plain mean. Some ghosts appear luminous, while others are shadowy or invisible. They may appear and disappear either suddenly or gradually. Some ghosts are nature spirits who enjoy playing pranks on humans. Still other ghosts are people who are dead but, for some reason, are still connected to the physical world. They may even be recognized by the people who see them.

It seems that ghosts are more easily observed through peripheral vision than by looking directly toward them. However, not everyone is able to see a ghost. Sometimes only one person in a group has eyes sensitive enough to do this. A ghostly experience doesn't need to be a visual one. Ghosts are sometimes heard and felt as well as seen. Sensing a presence is every bit as real as seeing a ghostly figure.

Believe me, it's not easy living with a ghost! For five months, our family had a ghost who took up residence in my seven-year-old son's bedroom. In the middle of the night, Scott would wake me up to tell me that there was someone in his room. I'm sorry to say that at first I didn't give much credence to his complaint and sent him back to his bed. Then I began to notice that Scott's room was much cooler than the rest of the house. One night, the Venetian blinds in his room started banging against the sill. I closed all his windows and locked them so there wasn't a breeze coming from outside. Still, night after night, the Venetian blinds banged back and forth. By this time, Scott was spending his nights in a sleeping bag on the floor of my bedroom. Then the strangest thing began to occur. Starting at the ceiling, little by little something was ripping the wallpaper off the wall in one-inch strips.

One night, my oldest son volunteered to sleep in Scott's room. He felt he was well equipped to meet a ghost face to face ... he had his boy scout knife with him. By midnight, he decided to go back to his own bedroom because someone kept pulling the covers off the bed as he was sleeping. Up to that point, I hadn't taken this whole experience seriously. All that changed after I spent a night in the haunted bedroom. One night made me a believer! I knew it was time for action. Because I had no experience with ghosts at that time, I called the local Catholic Church and asked for their help. But they replied that they didn't do exorcisms. Then I called the church where I was a member. Evidently they thought that I was either joking or crazy, because they hung up on me. Finally, I realized that it was up to me to get rid of our ghost.

I tried to make contact with the ghost — talking to it, asking questions, trying to find out what it wanted and how I could help. But there was no response. Then I got to work and moved all the furniture out and painted and repapered Scott's bedroom. Finally, after the room was redecorated, I took salt water and sprinkled the room with it. Then aloud I said, "From this day forth you are banished from this room and from this house. You are to go toward the light where you will find peace and love."

I had heard that before someone moves into a home it is wise to give it a spiritual housecleaning to clear out all negativity. So as a final step, I opened the closet doors. Then standing in the middle of Scott's room, I visualized white light completely filling the room. I continued the cleansing in every room in my house. Almost immediately I noticed that Scott's room was no longer colder than the rest of the house — no banging blinds, no rips in the wallpaper. Scott moved back into his room, and there was peace again in our home. Our unwanted guest was gone.

Was this just a stray ghost who decided to come for a visit? Was it a poltergeist? Perhaps it was the ghost of someone who had died in Scott's bedroom. The people from whom I purchased the house seemed a little strange and were very private. None of the neighbors knew anything about them. I have no answers, but I do know how it feels to be haunted by a ghost. It can be a scary experience. The stress had taken its toll on Scott. Our pediatrician diagnosed Scott's stomach pains as an ulcer. Ghosts cannot hurt anyone, but fear can!

Some hauntings are tied to a specific place, usually where a traumatic event occurred — for example, a battlefield or a murder scene. The haunting seems to replay sights and sounds like a tape that repeats over and over. A typical example might be the nightly footsteps heard in a hallway of an English castle, accompanied by the sound of rattling chains or the moans and screams of a victim from ages past. Hauntings may continue for years; however, several months may go by with no manifestation. The haunting may even skip certain tenants who never witness anything paranormal.

Rather than these hauntings being a manifestation of ghostly activity, it is more likely that they are thought forms that were created at the time the violence occurred. For example, when we hear the words "Oklahoma bombing," many of us picture a man walking away from the carnage with a bloody infant in his arms. That moment in time has been imprinted in the ether as well as in our minds. Strong emotions, such as fear or grief, give hauntings energy to continually replay the traumatic event.

"Poltergeist" is a German word meaning "noisy ghost." In the past, a poltergeist was thought to be either a demon or the spirit of someone who had died. Now some believe that they are probably mischievous nature spirits, which I call "imps," who are responsible for the activity. Perhaps they want to draw attention to themselves, or they just enjoy being malicious. Poltergeists' activities range from noises to violent destructiveness, from slamming doors or shattering dishes. Sometimes rocks pelt the walls, both inside and outside the house. At other times, objects mysteriously disappear and then later reappear. Sometimes fires are spontaneously ignited.

Often a poltergeist will throw an object, such as a knife or plate, in an aimless, erratic manner. Many times the object does not fly through the air but rather seems to be carried by an invisible hand. It moves more slowly than an object would travel if it had been thrown, and sometimes it even changes direction. Often the violence is centered around a specific member of the family, usually an adolescent. Generally the person is not aware that her pent-up energy can be used to energize the poltergeist and that, in a way, she is indirectly responsible for the action. Usually poltergeist activity is short-lived, but it can be quite violent while it lasts.

My encounter with a mischievous imp was many years ago. My teenage daughter and her friend were watching television while I was grading papers at my desk. Suddenly there was a loud crash. I looked up to see an imp sitting on my wrought-iron planter. He seemed quite pleased that he had been able to toss a fern from the top of my planter into the center of the living room. In a firm, angry voice, I told the imp to get out and never come back into my house again. Before our eyes, he began to shrink and gradually fade away. Thankfully, we never saw him again.

Because our pets have astral bodies, it is possible for them to become ghosts, especially if they don't realize that they are dead or if they are reluctant to leave their master. For several days after my beautiful sheltie, Ginger, died of a sudden heart attack, she lay in her astral body in her favorite place in the living room. Finally I realized that she did not know that she was dead, so I lovingly told her it was her time to leave. I do miss Ginger, but I realize that it is possible for her sweet spirit to come back to me sometime in the future within another dog's body.

It may seem strange to think of someone we have known as a ghost, but according to the dictionary, a ghost is the "disembodied soul of a dead person believed to be an inhabitant of the unseen world." "Disembodied" means "without a body," but we know that the person's consciousness and soul now resides in an astral body.

When a person dies, especially if the death has been sudden, permission is sometimes given for him to say goodbye or give a message to someone he was close to emotionally. Such spirits often appear wearing the same clothes and looking as they did at the time of their death. The ghostly visitation usually occurs at night while the living person is half asleep and half awake, in the alpha state. What may appear to be a dream could be an actual meeting with someone in the next dimension.

Bernice lost her eighteen-year-old son, Jimmy, in a tragic automobile accident one cold day in January. In the months that followed Jimmy's death, Bernice lay awake night after night trying to penetrate the veil that divides this world from the one beyond. She missed her son so deeply that all meaning had been drained from her life. Jimmy seemed so far away; he seemed lost forever. Then, five months after Jimmy's death, Bernice found him again. Even though Bernice was asleep, she knew it wasn't a dream. It was a real astral visit. Bernice and her son ran to each other and hugged. She laid her cheek against his chest. There was no trace of the wounds that had caused his death. "Jimmy, it's true then," said Bernice to her son. "There really is a Heaven, and you're alive and well." Her reunion with Jimmy was an important event. For the first time since his death, Bernice felt at peace about her loss.

When we see our loved one in a dream or a ghostly vision, it may not be just our imagination. It can be a real experience that takes place in an altered state of consciousness during meditation or sleep. Not everyone has a reunion dream. If you don't, it doesn't mean your love or loss is any less valid. For many people, a reunion conveys a message of reassurance that their deceased loved one is all right and that life does continue on the Other Side.

If the deceased has not experienced a lingering or debilitating death, it is possible for him to attend his own funeral celebration. My dad was very much in evidence at his funeral and seemed pleased that so many of his friends had come to honor him. For the reception following the funeral, I bought a beautiful cake inscribed with the words "Bon voyage, Fred." I suspect the baker would have been surprised to know the cake was for a funeral.

There are some people who claim that they have *captured* a ghost on film. It's extremely difficult to take a picture of a ghost because of their higher vibrations, but occasionally when the film is developed, a shadowy form or a ghostly face will appear on the print. Sometimes the face can be recognized as that of a deceased friend or relative. However, evaluating these pictures is very difficult because there are many ways that they can be faked. In the near future, as more sensitive film is produced, it may become much easier to take a picture of a relative or friend who is on the Other Side.

In the last few years progress has been made in taping ghostly voices from the next dimension. Even though the voices are faint and difficult to understand, scientists have been able to carry on conversations with astral citizens. As even more sensitive recording machines are invented, it may soon be possible to communicate with the astral world as easily as it is to use a telephone to make a long-distance call.

There are ghosts who, for one reason or another, refuse to accept the fact that they are dead and that it's time to leave the physical plane. Some are reluctant to leave the home or family to which they are deeply attached. Others believe that they have unfinished business to complete. These ghosts are often pathetic and confused. They seem to be frozen in time, trapped in an eerie space between the physical and astral worlds.

In the old days, people tried to placate a ghost with offerings of food. Sometimes they called on a witch doctor or shaman for help with a stubborn ghost. Now, if we want to get rid of an unwanted ghost, we may find it necessary to ask for assistance from a clergyman or a psychic. Often all the ghost needs is a firm but sympathetic push into the next dimension.

While I was living in the San Fernando Valley, a young woman phoned and asked for my help in getting rid of a ghost. She explained that she and her husband had purchased a small furnished house built in the early 1930s. The house had been put up for sale when the owner, an elderly widow, had died. Ever since the young couple had moved in, they had heard footsteps going from room to room. Then a rocking chair in their child's bedroom would start creaking as it rocked back and forth when no one was in the room.

The next day when I arrived at the house, the owner showed me the back bedroom where most of the ghostly activity was taking place. I sat on the bed and quietly started talking to the widow. I told her that she had died and that she no longer needed to stay in her home. I also explained that her husband was waiting for her on the Other Side, and it was time for her to cross over and be with him. For awhile longer I observed the chair rocking back and forth. Then it stopped. I felt that the elderly widow understood and was now ready to leave the physical plane. Several weeks later the young woman called to thank me and to report that there had not been any more evidence of a ghost in their house since my visit.

If you feel that your house is haunted, you need to do a thorough psychic housecleaning. I have found that one of the most effective ways to accomplish this is by going into each room of the house, opening closet doors and drawers, then ceremonially sprinkling salt water around the room. Next, with your eyes closed, visualize white light coming from your Higher Self and completely filling the room. Then you might say an affirmation — for example, "As the Light of God fills this room, all that is negative must depart and never return."

Occasionally a family discovers that having a ghost as a house guest is an experience that is more intriguing than scary. Some even begin to feel that the ghost has somehow become a member of the family.

So what do you do if, some night, you come face to face with a ghost? First and most important, remain as calm as possible. Remember that a ghost has no power to harm you, but fear can cause you a great deal of emotional distress. Next, try to determine what kind of ghost you are dealing with. If there has been a recent death of a friend or family member, try to communicate telepathically with the ghost to discover if there is some unfinished business or a personal message for you. If it's a poltergeist or mischievous spirit, be firm and demand that it leave you alone. The more we know about these ghostly inhabitants of the World Beyond the less likely we are to fear them.

7

Exploring the Lower Astral

As the students entered the college classroom, there was a feeling of excitement and an air of expectancy as they all found places to lay out their sleeping bags.

"Tonight," I told the students, "we are going to explore the lower astral planes. These lower planes lie partly on the surface of the earth and partly beneath it, interpenetrating the earth. Most of my former students have found that this section of the astral world is extremely unpleasant. I want you to be prepared for a negativity that is indescribable. Many of the inhabitants that we will encounter tonight will appear loathsome and completely lacking in spiritual love.

"The most common name for the lower astral is Hell. According to many religions, Hell is a place where the wicked go after death. There people will be punished for their wrongdoings. However, Cosmic Truth tells us that there is no such place as Hell, but that it is really a state of consciousness. While it is true that the lower planes of the astral world are bleak, dreary, and devoid of love, the truth is that we create Heaven or Hell every day of our lives through our thoughts and actions. Hell is being filled with negativity — hate, guilt, fear, anger, and revenge. Hell is the feeling of being separated from our Higher Self and not being worthy of the good that God wants to shower upon us. However, because so many people persist in their belief that Hell is a real place, it is reflected as such in the lower astral planes.

"Hindus, Buddhists, and Zoroastrians regard Hell as a temporary dwelling place where people are punished for their sins and then rehabilitated to prepare them to return in a physical body. Christians and Muslims picture Hell as a place of everlasting torment. Besides Hell, Catholics also believe in Purgatory, where good people who die must suffer and make amends for their sins before being admitted into Heaven.

"Gehenna became a synonym for Hell in Jewish, Islamic, and Christian tradition. Gehenna is the name of a valley southwest of Jerusalem. When I was in Israel, I visited this valley and was told that it had been the town dump, where trash was constantly burning, sending up thick smoke and emitting foul odors. As I have astrally traveled in the lower planes, I have found the atmosphere dense and smoggy, much like the trash dump in Gehenna.

"Another name for the lower astral is Hades. The kingdom of Hades was thought to be a neutral region reserved for the Souls of people who deserved neither punishment nor reward upon death. The Greeks believed that Hades was drab and dull, but not necessarily painful. They also believed that Hades was beneath the earth and that it had five rivers which served as a boundary between the land of the living and the dead. The Styx was the best known of these rivers. After crossing the river, they believed, each person was assigned to his proper eternal home.

"Many years ago I met weekly with a group of psychics and counselors in a beautiful home overlooking the San Fernando Valley. During that time we did rescue work. Our mission was to encourage those in the lower planes to ask for help and then to introduce them to their own Higher Self, or Guardian Angel, who fills the role of friend, teacher, and guide. We took turns: one of us would be used as a channel by an astral citizen while another acted as counselor. We were told that often those in the lower planes of the astral world related better to people who are in physical bodies than to the teachers from the higher planes.

"Before we leave on our astral adventure," I told the class, "I want to share with you two rescue sessions which I taped one evening. At the beginning of the tape are instructions channeled to us by a spiritual teacher from the Other Side." These began:

> *"Your most important mission is to let these poor Souls know that you love and care about them. Some will readily accept what you tell them and will be helped almost immediately. Others may scorn you and it will be difficult, or impossible, to give them any help. Are there any questions before we begin?"*
>
> "Yes. Who keeps order among the astral people who are waiting to be helped, and who chooses the ones who are to come through the channel?"
>
> *"We will keep order and lead the one that is to be helped into the body of the channel. People should not attempt rescue work unless they have been trained in counseling and have complete confidence in their Higher Self."*

The following are first-hand descriptions of what life is like in the lower astral planes given by the people who lived there:

"First somebody pushes me around this way and that and then they tell me to wait and I don't understand. Why do they keep pushing me around?"

"You won't be pushed around here. What is your name?"

" ... Mabel ... Yes, it's Mabel."

"Where do you live?"

"I just came here from where I've been. Is that what you mean?"

"Yes. Do you live someplace?"

"I don't have a place to live if you mean a house. No, I don't have a house to live in. People don't have houses over here."

"Well, you could have a house if you wish."

"You know what they do? They shove you here and they shove you over there. I mean, it's like we were a bunch of cattle."

"Is it crowded where you are?"

"We're just packed in, and it doesn't matter what you want to do. If they decide they want you over in this little part, then you get over to there. That's how I got here. They said, 'Okay, get over here.'"

"Don't you think it's about time you got out of there and had some freedom and a more beautiful place to live?"

"You mean, this isn't all there is? Oh, I've been longing for something better."

"Oh, there's a lot more, much more. Do you want to know how to ask for it?"

"Sure. I want to know."

"Ask to be taken into the light. That is the first step."

"Well, why can't I say I'd like the sunshine?"

"All right. Then ask for the sunshine."

"Because, you know, all there are are clouds. I mean, it doesn't rain, that's the funny thing. It doesn't rain but the clouds are always there. Now, what I was thinking .... I thought if they could just push the clouds away, then we could see the sun. I know the sun is up there. Now I want to push the clouds away."

"Then ask to have the clouds pushed away."

"How can I do it? I don't understand."

"Mabel, just ask. Ask for the light of the sun to shine down on you."

"Okay, I'll try ... Let the clouds go away and let the sun shine through ... it's getting lighter ... it really does work. I still don't understand, though."

"Now you can ask for someone to take you to a place where you won't be crowded or pushed around. Would you like to go to a rest home for a little while?"

"Rest homes are for the old or for people who are crazy. I'm not crazy. I'll tell you what I want ... I want to hold your hand. May I?" (The channel reaches over and holds the hand of the counselor.) *"You're so nice and warm."*

"Would you like to ask that someone come and lead you to a place where you can rest?"

"Yes ... Please come and take me away from here ... Oh, someone is coming towards me that shines like the sun ... Oh, I feel such love! Is this my new friend?"

"Yes. Your friend will take you to a place where you can have love and friendship. Nobody will push you around any more."

"I just don't understand this at all."

"You don't have to understand it right now to enjoy it, do you? Your new friend will answer all your questions when you are ready."

The following is the second recorded rescue mission:

"Hello, there. Would you like to talk to us? ... Can you tell us who you are?"

"I've been down here so long, I don't even know who I am."

"Can you tell us what year it is?" (This question was asked to find out how long she had been on the Other Side.)

"Oh, (shouting) *I don't know ... I've been drowning all these years. I don't know."*

"Are you male or female?"

"I'm a woman. Oh ..." (loud moaning).

"It's all right. You're no longer drowning."

"But the rocks are so slippery."

"Come up out of the water."

"But why did they put me there! Why did they do it to me?" (Screaming)

"First you need to come out of the muddy water and get clean."

"That's what I need. You know, that's what I need. I need to be clean. I need to get this slime off me."

"Ask to be clean. Just say, 'May I become completely clean?'"

"I need to be clean ... Do I have to go back into that slime?"

"No. Oh, no. You'll never have to be there again."

"I've been there forever. I don't understand."

"Are you getting clean?"

"It's coming off. But why did this happen to me? I didn't do anything."

"You'll get the answers later, but right now let's get you clean."

"Where am I?"

"You're in a home."

"Am I getting slime all over your rug?"

"It's all right. Can you tell us your name?"

"My name is Jill."

"Where do you live, Jill?"

"In the pit ... But I don't want to be there."

"You'll never have to be there again."

"Then where will I go?"

"If you look closely, you will see a bright, beautiful light. Do you see that light?"

"What's that noise?"

"It's our heater turning on."

"I need the heat. I'm so cold."

"You'll be getting warmer."

"But I don't understand why they put me there. I'm a good person."

"Your teacher and friend will answer your questions. Do you see the light?"

"I'm wrapped in the light ... I feel so warm."

"Good!"

"I don't want to slip and fall."

"You won't fall. Now ask to have a friend who will hold your hand and guide you to your new home."

"Please ... I want someone to take me to a

new home where it's warm ... Did they think I was bad?"

"You'll understand soon. Your teacher and friend will answer your questions."

"Why are you here?"

"Because we love you and we want to help you."

"Oh, thank you. I didn't know anyone loved me. I'm so happy."

"Is the teacher standing by your side a man or woman?"

"I don't know. (Laughs). *He isn't wearing pants. It looks like he is wearing a robe."*

"Reach out your hand and ask to be taken to your new home."

"Okay. I want to go to my new home ... Thank you. Gee, thank you so much ... Goodbye."

"Goodbye, Jill. We won't forget you."

After I stopped the tape recorder, I told the students, "Our group of spiritual counselors felt a deep sense of satisfaction when we were able to help those in the lower astral planes find a better way of life. Of course teachers from the higher planes are always available for counseling, but nothing can actually be done until the tormented person asks for help. When they ask for help and become aware of their spiritual teacher, then they will be released from their self-created Hell and take a step forward in their development.

"Now we are ready to start our exploration of the World Beyond. Close your eyes and breathe deeply. Relax your physical body. (See chapter 1 for the complete procedure.) Visualize an astral elevator with its doors open. See yourself entering the elevator. The doors close and we are taken into the lower planes of the astral world."

The sight that greets us as the elevator doors open is not a pleasant one. The scene is reminiscent of a shanty-town spread out over a barren desert. The land is rocky and the earth is parched.

The few people whom we see are sitting alone, making no attempt to communicate with any of the other inhabitants. Their dirty, tattered clothes appeared to be the ones they were wearing when they arrived. Many look as if they are starving to death because they think that they need food to continue existing. Some make lewd gestures or vulgar remarks as we walk past. These lower astral planes are inhabited by people almost totally devoid of love.

A Higher Being, looking very much like a sheriff, walks over to us and tells our group, "I will be your guide for today. You will find every imaginable suffering possible is reflected here in the lower planes. The suffering seems very real to those who are going through this experience. If people believe that Hell is a burning fire, this is what they will experience, because life in the astral world is a reflection of the mind.

"Probably the best description of the lower planes was found engraved on a stone by an ancient Egyptian writer: 'What manner of foul region is this ... Souls wander hopelessly and helplessly about; in it there is no peace, no calm, no rest, no quiet of the heart or mind.'"

One of the students asks our guide, "How does God judge what plane in the astral world we are sent to when we leave the physical world through death?"

The Higher Being answers, "God does not sit on a throne and judge anyone. When you leave the physical world through death, with the guidance of your Higher Self, you are your own judge and jury. Thus, the concept of reward and punishment is a matter of vibratory reaction to our actions. The vibrations of punishment include guilt, worry, anger, hatred, and fear. People indeed suffer as they think they should. Their agony and pain cannot be relieved until they realize that they themselves have decreed their own torment."

Another student asks, "Have all those in the lower planes left their physical bodies through death?"

Our guide replies, "Sometimes people who are having an out-of-body experience inadvertently stumble into the lower planes of the World Beyond, perhaps because of a drug overdose or an alcoholic stupor. They become very confused because they can see things that other people can't see. They can hear voices that no one else can hear. Some mental illnesses are defined as seeing, hearing, or sensing something that does not really exist. It seems that many in the medical profession do not understand what is really happening. True, these sights and sounds do not exist in the physical world, but they are very real and are happening in the astral world. Somehow, these people are experiencing the confusing world of the lower astral planes.

"Because the lower planes are so closely connected to the physical world," our guide continues, "it is possible for some astral citizens who miss their drugs or liquor to hang around bars and high-crime areas where these are being used. They are waiting to literally take possession of some unsuspecting person who has overdosed or is extremely drunk. In this way, these lower astral inhabitants can vicariously experience the rush of alcohol or drugs."

For awhile longer our group wanders down the dusty roads, observing the inhabitants and their seeming lack of interest in what is happening around them. Finally it is time to leave the lower planes and return to the physical world. Two members of our class felt nauseated by the negativity, and we all agree that we are more than ready to leave these lower planes. As we prepare to depart, we are requested to stand under a spiritual shower where any negativity that we might have inadvertently picked up will be washed away. Then we enter the astral elevator and are once again back in our classroom. The students are quiet for a longer time than usual before sharing their experiences and reactions with the rest of the class. Everyone agrees that they have no desire to spend any more time in the lower astral planes.

8

Extraterrestrials in Our Midst

One of the most exciting astral adventures that the students in my classes experience is traveling to an astral spaceship. Many of the students have a background in the sciences, so I usually begin by explaining to them, "There are a group of astronomers who have devoted their careers to locating and taking photographs of Earth-like planets outside our solar system. Some of them believe that there may be life out there that is intelligent enough to transmit radio signals across vast stretches of space. These can be received by the Billion-channel Extra Terrestrial Assay (or BETA) receiver near Boston. Here all incoming radio waves are fed into a supercomputer that sorts through the input and discards cosmic noise as it searches for a message from outer space. As more planets are discovered in other solar systems, scientists reason that at least some of them will fall into a habitable zone where water is liquid rather than solid or gas. These bio-friendly planets may be more abundant than astronomers have previously suspected. The time is coming when they will finally have proof that there is indeed intelligent life in the universe.

"Never before have extraterrestrials made such a profound impact on the inhabitants of Earth as they are doing in our generation. In the skies above Earth, thousands of people have seen the spacecraft perform feats that no airplane could possibly duplicate. Our scientists and our governments know this, but they file their reports in secret and tell the public that they have seen a weather balloon or some kind of a natural phenomenon. The same government agencies that swear that UFOs do not exist have tons of classified information to prove otherwise. Why do governments need secret files on something that doesn't exist and then refuse to release these files on the grounds that national security is at risk? Pilots who have first-hand knowledge about the spacecraft have been silenced under the threat of losing their jobs and their retirement pay."

The appearance of spacecraft in all the skies of our world provides overwhelming evidence that ours is not the only inhabited planet in the universe. We will soon have proof that Earth is only one of innumerable inhabited planets in this vast, orderly universe.

Extraterrestrials have been interested in Earth since the beginning of time as we know it. They have come from other planets in our solar system and even from distant galaxies. Some of these extraterrestrials came to Earth as refugees from a planet that was in danger of being destroyed. Others were outcasts and renegades who were banned from their home planets and exiled to Earth. Settlers arrived from other planets to establish colonies. Great Masters came to teach the Earthians a better way of life. These men and women from other worlds came into physical form not only to share their expertise in every field of endeavor but also to help lift the spiritual vibrations of Earth. The early races of humans called these Masters "gods" and "goddesses." Whether we call them "gods and goddesses," "masters," "aliens," or "renegades," we recognize the fact that these extraterrestrials are scientifically more advanced than we are on Earth.

In ancient times some human beings were believed to have had a divine or extraterrestrial father and a mortal mother. Those who were part god and part human were called "heroes." Tradition tells us that many of the great Masters and Avatars were born of an extraterrestrial father and an Earth mother. The rulers of many ancient civilizations — including Egyptian pharaohs, Sumerian kings, Persian rulers, and Japanese emperors — were also believed to be direct descendants of the gods.

Most stories concerning divine beings attributed supernatural powers to them. But in spite of their powers, many of the gods and goddesses had human characteristics. They not only resembled human beings but also expressed human emotions such as love, hate, jealousy, and anger. So we shouldn't be at all surprised when extraterrestrials exhibit human personality traits.

Sometimes extraterrestrials have lowered the vibrations of their spacecraft, enabling them to be observed by humans. An ancient Indian epic, the *Mahabharata*, describes flying machines that navigated at great heights with the aid of quicksilver and a great wind. These flying machines covered vast distances and could travel upward and downward as well as forward and backward. Sumerian, Assyrian, Babylonian, and Egyptian inscriptions all present the same story of gods and goddesses who came from the stars and went back to them. They traveled through the heavens in fireships and possessed amazing weapons. The translation of an ancient Sanskrit text reads in part: "An apparatus that moves by inner strength like a bird either on earth, in the water, or in the air, is called Vimana. It can move in the sky from place to place, from world to world. The building of these flying machines that stand still or become invisible is kept secret."

The Bible, the Epic of Gilgamesh, and many other

ancient sources also tell of flying gods in strange heavenly vehicles. Among the scrolls found at the Dead Sea we read about heavenly chariots that had wheels of fire, and every wheel was "full of eyes all around." Tibetan books mention prehistoric flying machines which were called "pearls in the sky."

Old texts and archeological discoveries around the world indicate that the first spacecraft observed above our planet were spherical. A sphere has no fore or aft, no right or left, and offers the same surface in every position and direction; therefore, it is the ideal shape for the smaller spaceships. Most of the spacecraft seen today are the same type observed during ancient times. Only the descriptive terminology has changed.

Nothing is more convincing than seeing a spacecraft with your own eyes. It's an experience that one never forgets. The first time I had the privilege of seeing a spaceship, a group of us were enjoying a summer picnic. As the sun went down and the stars became brighter, two of us noticed a spacecraft as it darted back and forth and then disappeared before our eyes. The rest of the group were unable to see anything unusual. The reason that some can see the spaceships while others cannot is that some people's eyes are more attuned to the higher vibrations.

In 1971 I was teaching fourth grade in the San Fernando Valley. It was afternoon and I was taking my class out for physical education when some of the children noticed what appeared to be the Goodyear blimp hovering over the mountains to the east of our playground. We were all watching it in fascination when it began slowly to disappear right before our eyes. By that time the children and I had realized that it was not a blimp after all, but a real UFO. The spacecraft had raised its vibrations from the third to the fourth dimension and had become invisible.

One morning when my friend Eva Marie and I were vacationing at Mt. Shasta, we left the little log cabin we were renting and headed into town for breakfast. As we turned south, there directly in front of us was a spacecraft shining against a bright blue sky. I quickly pulled over to the side of the road, and Eva Marie jumped out of the car and took several pictures. Imagine our disappointment when the pictures were developed and, instead of a spaceship, there were only clouds. Even though we could see it, the vibrations of the spacecraft were too high to be photographed. Over the years, some photos and video tapes have been taken of spaceships. As more sensitive film is produced, it will become easier to capture a spacecraft on film.

A year after I moved to Eugene, Oregon, I was telepathically told that on Monday evening, at 10:00 p.m., a spacecraft would fly by my home. I had never heard of any space people making an appointment, but I am a believer, so I invited a dozen friends to my home that Monday evening. About 9:55 p.m., we all went outside on my front deck and began to scan the sky. To the south, I noticed an exceptionally bright star. As we watched, a small disc came down from the star and grew closer and larger. It moved slowly and silently until it was over the treetops at the edge of my ranch. It was close enough for us to see the circular portholes in the spacecraft. We were all speechless and our hearts were pounding. We thought that perhaps it might land in the pasture, but it continued moving slowly toward the north until it was out of sight. We stood there on the deck in silence for awhile. When we finally expressed our thoughts, we all agreed that we had just shared a very spiritual experience.

There are thousands of spaceships operating in our solar system at all times. There is a great deal of activity as the small scout craft move about carrying out their surveying activities and other duties. Large mother ships are stationed far above Earth for long periods of time, keeping track of our planet on their monitoring equipment. These larger craft are capable of visiting planets in other solar systems, because they travel in a higher dimension where time and space are not as we understand them in the third dimension.

It has been more than twenty years since I met an astral space person for the first time. After a long day of teaching school, my friend Cynthia and I were both exhausted. We decided that it would help us to unwind if we could quietly meditate together for a few minutes. But we had a problem. Cynthia and I both had houses full of children, and it would be difficult to have any privacy or quiet time if we went to either of our homes. So Cynthia suggested that we go to a nearby chapel that was open during the day.

We had been in the chapel only a short while, quietly meditating, when we became aware that we were not alone. There in his astral body stood a tall, lean man dressed in a tight-fitting, one-piece suit made of a shiny gold material. Both Cynthia and I were startled, but we knew by his vibrations of love that he would not harm us. He telepathically introduced himself as "Octavia" and said he had a message for us:

> *"You have been chosen to be intermediaries between the Earthians and members of the Intergalactic Fleet. It will be your assignment to help Earthians to become more aware of their mission on Earth and less fearful of the changes which will be occurring. You are to awaken those*

who have volunteered to join us so they will be physically and emotionally prepared to be beamed aboard one of our ships."

Having given this message, he abruptly faded from our astral sight, leaving Cynthia and me with a lot of unanswered questions. We weren't sure what our responsibilities would be, but I have taken the assignment as an intermediary seriously. Over the years I have been active in helping people to understand extraterrestrials.

After our first meeting, I kept in touch astrally with Octavia as he was promoted from junior officer and later given command of his own ship. One day, my close friend Margaret and I were meditating together when Octavia suddenly appeared astrally and telepathically informed us that on Monday, around noon, someone from a spacecraft would physically meet with us at my friend's home. We were excited because we had not seen a space person in a physical body before.

On the appointed day, I drove to Margaret's home. As I approached the freeway offramp, I noticed a black car right behind me. The car followed me off the freeway and continued behind me as I turned on several streets and parked in the driveway of my friend's home. I really hadn't paid that much attention until the car parked directly across the street. I could see two men in the front seat dressed in black suits and wearing black hats. Now in southern California, that in itself is strange.

When I went inside, I told Margaret about being followed by the black car, which was now parked across from her house. Through the curtains we watched the men sitting in their car. In a few minutes we heard loud knocking on her front door. Both of us were too frightened to answer the door. The men in black sat in their car for about half an hour before driving away. They had evidently accomplished their mission, because we never did see the physical space visitor who was to contact us.

The stories of men in black date back to at least 1953, when Albert Bender of Bridgeport, Connecticut, claimed he had been visited by three men dressed in black suits. He said that they revealed to him the secrets of spaceships but that they also intimated that he'd end up in jail if he told anyone. Later he warned other people who were investigating the UFO phenomenon to be very cautious about publicizing their findings lest the men in black become involved. Since that time there have been many reports of men dressed in black clothes who have threatened or warned people connected with UFO research. Thus, they became known as the "men in black," or "MIB." They usually travel in twos or threes, often arriving or departing in black Cadillacs or other large black sedans.

These men in black sometimes indicate that they are government agents or military intelligence officers. They have been known to appear on a UFO witness's doorstep before the person has had a chance to report a sighting. The men demand all photographic negatives and other UFO evidence while warning the witness to keep quiet about what he may have seen or heard. Who are these men in black? Are they really military intelligence officers or government agents? Or are they extraterrestrials who are interested in suppressing certain information? Whoever they are, there has never been a reported case where they have physically harmed anyone.

Some extraterrestrials want to make their presence known in a nonthreatening manner, so they have been creating circular patterns in fields, especially in England. In one summer, more than four hundred of these crop circles appeared, almost always at night. Inside each perfectly formed circle, the plants lie bent but not broken, with the still-growing stalks swept into a matted, pinwheel pattern. If a circle is laid down early in the season, the rapidly growing stalks soon pick themselves up and grow straight again. Viewed from the air, many of the circles form complex patterns. Although circles have been seen in parts of the United States, Canada, and Australia, most have occurred in southern England.

The phenomenon of crop circles has been occurring over a long period of time. Many legends from the Middle Ages refer to large circles that formed in the fields overnight. Back then, people talked of fairies dancing through the corn or of devils who came in the night and cut rings in the crops. But over the centuries, crop circles were only occasionally seen and rarely reported. Now, because it is possible to view them from the air and because of the publicity, more and more crop circles are being found. As the designs become more elaborate, some believe that they contain coded information which will help to trigger hidden soul memories. Some believe that the extraterrestrials use a pattern, something like a template, and a strong electromagnetic energy field to create their art work in the fields of Earth.

It is important that we are aware of the different types of extraterrestrials who are interested in Earth and her inhabitants. There are at least three distinct groups with very different motives for their interest. I have named them the "Scientific group," the "Renegades," and the "Spiritual group."

The first group, as the name implies, has a scientific interest in Earth. These space scientists are here neither to assist nor to harm the people of Earth but are merely interested in increasing their scientific knowledge. They are carrying out a variety of experiments and are collecting data about Earth and its inhabitants. Many of these scientists are geniuses, and the information that they are gathering is of a highly intellectual nature. They may be experimenting with crossbreeding and may also be interested in colonizing Earth. The extraterrestrial scientists use humanoids to carry out their experiments. These humanoids have been referred to as "Grays" because of their pallid skin. They are short in stature, with oversized heads, thin limbs, and large eyes. The Grays are not what we would consider human but are more like technically advanced robots.

The scientific extraterrestrials are probably responsible for the mutilation of cattle in the western United States. When the carcass is discovered, it is completely drained of blood. The sexual organs and other parts of the animal's body have been surgically removed with laser-like precision. Sometimes hovering lights have been observed, but otherwise there is not a single clue to how the mutilation of the cattle was accomplished.

Because these space scientists are interested in humans, they may be giving astral or physical exams to certain people. Many otherwise ordinary individuals claim that they were kidnapped by extraterrestrials and taken aboard a spacecraft. They were usually released within a few hours with little or no memory of what occurred — but always there is a feeling that something strange took place. Some victims express pain, sorrow, or terror because of their experiences. Many feel shaken and humiliated, with nobody to turn to for help. The trauma, which has been compared to post-traumatic stress disorder, results when the person's experience does not fit into society's mode of reality.

Under hypnosis, the abductees are able to remember seeing gray humanoids who were about four feet tall. They had huge bald heads, elongated eyes, flattened noses, slit mouths, and narrow shoulders. The abductees tell of suddenly feeling immobile and being given a physical examination. Some remembered long needles being stuck into their abdomens, eyes, or nostrils. Sometimes during the medical exam, samples of eggs or sperm were removed. Some reported feeling sharp pain that vanished with a wave of an alien's hand.

Most of the people I have met who believe they have been abducted appear confused and fearful. Have these people really been taken aboard a spacecraft? In my talks with them, I explain that during our sleep state, we experience several different types of dreams. One kind of dream replays things that we have experienced during the day, including movies or television shows we have watched. It is possible that some people are tuning into their dreams about space people and UFOs and are taking them literally.

Another type of dream is really not a dream at all but an actual astral experience during which we leave the sleeping physical body behind and go exploring in the astral body. It is possible that this exploration could lead us to a spaceship. The subconscious and superconscious minds are aware of everything we are experiencing, but the conscious mind is aware of only a part of what is happening and may be confused by an astral adventure. To some people, astral travel can seem as real as a physical experience. Many people have reported that they were frightened or frustrated when they tried to move the physical body but couldn't. They didn't realize that they were still out in the astral body while the physical body was asleep.

Other people I have talked with consider themselves to be "contactees" and tell of being on board a large, disc-shaped craft where they met tall space beings who were light-haired and light-skinned and looked very much like humans. They said that they felt a tremendous amount of love and tranquility while on board the spacecraft. These contactees reported that their experience with extraterrestrials had been uplifting. Whether people feel that they were victims of an abduction or that they were privileged to be contactees, on a higher level permission was given for the experience by the Higher Self.

A second type of extraterrestrials are the Renegades who belong to the Dark Forces. Their motive is to take over Earth and rule as conquerors. Those of the Dark Forces have been causing problems since the early days of Earth. Many ancient writings mention wars and battles in the heavens. The Egyptian *Book of the Dead* tells how the mighty sun god, Ra, fought with the rebellious children in the universe. A Sanskrit translation from the *Book of Dzyan* reads: "There were battles fought between the creators and the destroyers, and battles fought for space." In Revelations it is written: "Then there was war in heaven; Michael and the angels under his command fought the Dragon and his hosts of fallen angels. And the Dragon lost the battle and was forced from heaven." Maori legends of the South Seas tell of a rebellion that broke out in heaven after Tane had arranged the stars. Those who were no longer willing to follow Tane he smote with lightning; he conquered the insurgents and threw them down to Earth.

If there were wars in the universe, then there must have been conquerors and conquered. Did the victors remain in possession of their own planet? Did the defeated have to flee? The rival parties probably had the same knowledge, experience, and technological development. Perhaps the defeated group, having escaped from the battle in spaceships, had to find a planet similar to their home planet. Perhaps the losers found Earth a safe refuge from the victors.

Those of the Dark Forces have been called "fallen angels," "rebellious children," "destroyers," or "renegades." They are openly opposed to the spiritual space beings and would seize our planet if given a chance. They would control it for their own purposes, ruling as dictators and doing away with our free will. Some of the renegades have been described as reptilian, but for generations they have called Earth their home and have incarnated in physical bodies until they now resemble us. However, their thoughts and actions are still negative. They are evil in their intent, because anyone who deliberately hurts another individual is evil. Those of the Dark Forces are few in number, but their strength is great.

What is taking place on our planet at this time is a battle for control. Those of the Dark Forces are using their negative power to control and intimidate, and create a fear-based consciousness on planet Earth. Some believe that the Renegades have created a secret world government through which they will try to control all Earth's leaders. Most of the leaders of our world are unaware of this secret government and its negative power. It is up to us to help defeat the secret government of the Dark Forces. We can accomplish this by individually expressing peace and love on a personal level. Our combined energy of peace and love will then manifest in the world in which we live.

It is important that we are able to recognize those of the Dark Forces who are physically living among us. The method of determining who is friend and who is foe is through their vibrations. The vibrations of the Renegades are negative and oppressive, which creates a feeling of fear or impending doom. We need to remember that the negative vibration of fear attracts negative experiences, while the vibration of love destroys fear. The best protection we have against these negative extraterrestrials is the White Light of God coming through our Higher Self. When in doubt, ask to be surrounded with this White Light. The spiritual extraterrestrials will welcome it; the Renegades will leave you alone. A warning has been given from the Intergalactic Council not to approach or board a space ship that has landed because, up to this time, only scientific extraterrestrials and Renegades have landed on Earth.

The Intergalactic Council has decreed that those of the Dark Forces who have not been willing or able to raise their vibrations through unconditional love will no longer be allowed to incarnate repeatedly on planet Earth. When they die, they will be sent to another planet where they will be given an opportunity to learn the lessons they have failed to learn in their sojourn on Earth. Without their negativity, Earth can become a planet of love and peace.

Extraterrestrials of the third type belong to the Spiritual Hierarchy. My experiences have only been with these space people, who are responsible citizens of the cosmos. They love Earth and are here to protect and help Earthians. They have girdled Earth with their ships to form a resonant field that will assist our planet as we prepare to make a quantum leap into the fourth dimension.

On several occasions I have had the privilege of astrally meeting Ashtar, who is the commander of the Intergalactic fleet serving the Western Hemisphere. He is almost seven feet tall, with piercing blue eyes and pale hair and skin. A tremendous amount of strength radiates from him when I have channeled his message. Ashtar affirms that despite those who plot and plan otherwise, if we all work together, Earth, along with the other planets in our solar system, will become a member of the Universal Alliance for peace.

The high-ranking officers on board the spiritual spaceships are what we would term "angels"; they are androgynous beings of pure love. Their whole purpose for being here is to help us raise Earth's vibrations into the fourth dimension. Ascended Masters from Earth and men and women of other evolved worlds are also aboard the spiritual spacecraft.

The mission to planet Earth involves millions of spaceships, from the small scout craft to giant, city-sized mother ships. These mother ships are anchored high in our atmosphere, and each can accommodate thousands of people. The world has been divided into sections or sectors, and a mother ship is stationed above each sector. All headquarters operations are carried out in them. The scout crafts arrive here from other planets and other solar systems, carried by the mother ships. These interplanetary space stations exist in another dimension at a different frequency and are not limited by our time coordinates. Spaceships travel from planet to planet and solar system to solar system in a higher dimension. This makes it possible for them to travel faster than the speed of light. They can be transported from place to place almost instantaneously.

It has been predicted that a day will come when a physical body can be reduced to a stream of electrons, then beamed to a distant point and reassembled. Science has now proven that mass can be converted into energy and back into mass again. Our space neighbors have been using this method of transport for a very long time. Indeed, some of the things that are shown on *Star Tre*k are more fact than fiction.

While our physical bodies have slept, many of us have astrally sat in on Intergalactic Council meetings and listened to the plans for Earth over the next ten years. Although we may not be consciously aware of what has been discussed, all the information has been stored in the subconscious mind. The members of the Intergalactic Council are a powerful force for good, but they are not allowed to interfere with the free will of the people of Earth. The Council does, however, have the authority to intervene in any planetary situation that threatens widespread destruction, such as a nuclear war.

Since we have been given free will, we have the freedom to express evil as well as good. The choice whether our planet and its people will transcend this critical period in Earth's evolution and raise our vibrations to the fourth dimension is a choice that we all must make collectively as well as individually.

A lot of planning and hard work has gone into this mission to prepare Earth for the coming new age. There are millions of extraterrestrials involved with the mission, while millions of people on Earth are consciously or unconsciously cooperating in the program. Everyone of us has a part to play in this important drama in Earth's history. We need the help of extraterrestrials and humans alike to bring forth Earth's Golden Age of Peace.

9

On Board a Spacecraft

"I have a surprise for you this evening," I told the class. "We will be taking an astral ride in a spacecraft. Some of you may have already traveled astrally to one of the large spaceships stationed above our Earth while you were asleep, but most do not remember the experience. Now is the time for you to explore the spacecraft while consciously traveling astrally so that you can become more familiar with the ship itself."

Jim, one of the members of our class, seemed genuinely disturbed and said, "I'm not sure I want to go on a flying saucer to meet a bunch of aliens. When you see them in the movies and on TV, many of them are ugly, hostile, and bent on conquering the Earth. I'm afraid they might try to keep us up there."

"First, let me say to all of you that there is nothing to fear," I replied. I then explained to them the difference between the renegades and the scientific and spiritual extraterrestrials. Then I told them, "I have only had contact with the spiritual extraterrestrials who are our space brothers and sisters. Their only interest is to be of help to us and to our planet. Jim, I also need to say that they really dislike the terms 'flying saucer' and 'aliens,' so it is best not to use those words."

"Now I want you to get comfortable, relax, close

your eyes, and yawn a couple of times. As I count from one to twenty, you will go deeper and deeper into the alpha state." By now, most of the members of the class were finding it easier to enter the alpha state and to leave their physical bodies and travel astrally.

When our tour group was ready, I telepathically requested an astral scout craft to come and transport us to a mother ship. In a very short time, the ship was hovering above our classroom. A stairway ramp was lowered, and we astrally boarded the spaceship. When we were seated in swivel chairs and our seat belts were fastened, we were ready to begin our adventure. Our pilot, seated at the controls in the center of the craft, closed the sliding doors with a flick of a switch. As we lifted off, there was only a soft hum and a slight feeling of movement, but no sense of acceleration. We would hardly have known that we were moving unless we had looked out one of the portholes and seen Earth receding below us.

I would judge that the craft was about fifteen feet in diameter. The comfortable swivel chairs circled the outside wall. There was a soft glow in the cabin, but I did not see any light fixtures. In the center of the cabin was the pilot's circular instrument panel, filled with all sorts of knobs, switches, colored lights, and vision screens. The pilot told us that at both the top and bottom of the craft are powerful, wide-angle periscopes with sensors which not only send pictures to the vision screen but also sound a warning if an aircraft is approaching.

In a surprisingly short time we could see the mother ship. As we got closer, we were amazed at its tremendous size. Our pilot skillfully guided the scout craft into a landing airlock. When the doors of the airlock closed behind us, doors in front opened. Now we were on a moving ramp and our ship was attached to a cable which pulled us forward into a large hangar. When we stopped at an unloading dock, the door of the scout craft slid open and we prepared to disembark.

Before we left the ship, I told the students, "Each of you will be met by a guide. You may discover that it is someone you know from a past life, or it might even be an android. It's difficult to tell an android from a space person because they appear quite human. The difference is that androids are not ensouled and are really not alive as we know life to be. They are well fitted for work on the mother ship, since they have no physical or emotional needs."

While we were waiting for our guides, a maintenance officer came over to our group and told us, "There's always a lot of action in this huge hangar as we work on the ships to get them ready for their next flight. You can probably understand this better if you compare our ship to one of your aircraft carriers. Airplanes not only take off and land on a carrier but are transported long distances aboard the ship. Large elevators move the planes from the landing deck to the huge hangar and storage decks. A carrier provides living quarters for the pilots, air crew, ship's crew, and other personnel. There is also a large, well-equipped repair shop on board. Our mother ship is very much like one of your aircraft carriers. We also have a large machine shop, because even on a spaceship parts break down, and it is important to keep everything in perfect flying condition."

The officer continued, "Our scout craft are not capable of generating their own power, so they can make only relatively short trips from the mother ship before they need recharging. We use them as a shuttle service between the large ships and to and from Earth, but they are always dependent on the power plant aboard the mother ship."

Just then our hostess arrived with her group of guides and said, "On behalf of the captain and myself, I welcome you on board. Please feel free to ask your guide any questions that you may have. You may also request to see any particular part of the ship that is of special interest to you. We will all meet in the recreation room in about an hour."

Usually one of the first places to visit on our tour is a stateroom. They are not large but are well equipped to meet every physical need. The bed is built in with storage space below. When I sat down, I thought it was a water bed, but my guide informed me it is even better: it is an air bed. The furnishings consist of a simple desk chair, an end table with storage beneath, and an extremely comfortable recliner chair covered in a beautiful plush material. There is a large mirror/viewing screen above the vanity/desk. This viewing screen, which is probably three by four feet, makes it possible not only to receive the latest news, movies, and training films, but also to be visually in touch with anyone on board. The walls and ceiling of the stateroom are white, but with a turn of a dial you can "paint" the stateroom any color you choose by a special method of indirect lighting.

Because those on board the spaceships are either fourth- or fifth-dimensional or androids, they have no need for food. Now for the first time, the space people are faced with the challenge of preparing to feed the people from Earth when they are beamed aboard, because their physical bodies still need nourishment. The space farmers are very proud of what they have accomplished through the science of hydroponics, a technique in which plants are suspended with their roots in water to which nutrients have been added. The space farmers have worked out the correct amount of artificial light and warmth necessary to grow the crops. On board the ship, the menu will be vegetarian, with little variety but good nutritional value.

The men in our class were interested in the operational part of the mother ship. A ship's officer explained to us, "Our craft is operated through reversible electromagnetism. A crystal-like rotor in the center of the ship is linked to two large columns which are the reactors. Reversing magnetic and electrical energy makes it possible to control matter and overcome the forces of gravity."

Because I know nothing about what makes engines run, it was difficult for me to comprehend his explanation, but I listened intently, hoping I could understand part of what he was telling our group.

The officer continued, "Our spacecraft generate their own gravitational field, which causes them to become almost weightless. Because of this, a ship can move through space by using a relatively slight thrust. By using advanced technology, we are able to raise or lower the vibrations of the ship. As the energy is increased we can travel at speeds faster than light. When a spaceship accelerates and seems to disappear, it is vibrating at a speed faster than the visible portion of the spectrum, thus becoming invisible to people on Earth. Our ships use solar and crystal power which can be used either separately or together. Our spacecraft are made of lightweight, heat-resistant metal, as thin as aluminum foil but stronger than any metal known on Earth."

As the officer led the way to the ship's control center, the door parted in the middle and slid into the wall, just as I have seen it on *Star Trek*. In the control room, we met two crew members who, like the officer, were tall and slim with light skin and blond hair. They were dressed in what appeared to be a one-piece, dark blue jumpsuit. These men were sitting at a large console filled with many screens and dials. We were shown a master computer that links this ship to all of the other craft in the fleet. We were also shown a disc-shaped object about six feet in diameter. They explained that this is used for remote-controlled reconnaissance and surveillance. It transmits pictures back to the vision screen on the mother ship.

The ship's infirmary far surpasses any medical facility on Earth. The medications and the healing techniques of light and sound are very effective. The last time I was astrally on board, the medical officer, a bright young woman, spoke to us briefly and then suggested that we all get shots. I never did find out why we needed them.

An hour had gone by, and it was time to meet in the recreation area. To me, this is the most interesting place on the whole ship. Here you will find every imaginable type of equipment to keep your physical and emotional bodies healthy. There is an exercise and weight room, a sauna, and a large assortment of nearly life-size video games. There are individual rooms where you can experience a mini-vacation complete with sight and sound. You can pick the vacation you want: seashore, mountain stream, forest, meadow, and more. I chose the seashore, where I was surrounded by visual and sound effects: the waves were breaking on the rocks; there was a tang of salt in the air; several sea gulls were circling overhead, and the sun was warm on my body. A mini-vacation provides a pleasant respite from the limited space and daily routine aboard the ship.

The members of our class really seemed to enjoy themselves in the recreation room. Finally a young woman asked us to follow her to the lounge to meet one of the ship's captains. The lounge was large and beautifully decorated. Although no light fixtures were visible, the whole room was filled with a soft blue-white light. The thick wall-to-wall carpet was in various shades of green and blue. Arranged in groups around the room was an assortment of divans and chairs covered in a plush material in colors which harmonized with the carpet. On the tops of the variously shaped end tables was a material that looked like crystal. I was especially drawn to several landscapes hanging on the wall. There were pictures of the beach, mountains, and a field of wildflowers. Each picture had water that appeared to be moving, in the form of either an ocean, a waterfall, or a little stream. These pictures were exceedingly beautiful but difficult to describe.

When all the students were comfortably seated, the captain entered the lounge. He was tall and had the bearing of someone in authority. His one-piece suit looked like spun gold, and his powerful voice filled the room as he spoke to us. "Many of you are being prepared for a special mission. You may not be consciously aware of this mission, but on the inner levels, you have an expectant attitude. Before you incarnated, you made some very important decisions concerning the role you are to play in helping your planet during this exciting time in Earth's history. For those who have raised their vibrations, there are three options. Some, through death, will go into the higher dimension. Others have chosen to be survivors and remain on the Earth plane. Still others have chosen to be beamed aboard a spacecraft. Look deep within your hearts and you will know whether or not you have volunteered to be a part of this mission.

"Those who have chosen to leave the physical body through death will be given an opportunity to become involved in intensive training in astral universities, preparing them to return to Earth again through birth. Many of these people will choose to incarnate quickly so that they can participate more fully in positions of leadership. Others who have attained Mastership may feel that their work on Earth has been completed and will choose not to return.

"Probably the most difficult option is to be one of the survivors who will remain on Earth as your planet makes a quantum leap into the fourth dimension. It will not be an easy choice. Those who plan to stay will need to be physically, emotionally, and mentally strong. These survivors, with the help of their Higher Self, will be leaders and counselors in the new age. People who are confused or afraid will look to them for help and guidance.

"Some of you have chosen to be beamed aboard a spacecraft. I know a few people who are eagerly looking forward to this experience since they believe that they will be lifted up out of the problems and poverty they have created for themselves on Earth. They have forgotten that their mission is to create Heaven on Earth and not just to mark time until they can leave.

"The cosmic plan is to lift off individuals as natural disasters increase. If this is your choice, you will be physically beamed aboard one of the hundreds of spaceships that are stationed in the skies above Earth. In order to survive this experience, your body must be in excellent physical health. You will also need to have attained a high degree of Soul evolvement and spiritual growth. You will need to be mentally alert and emotionally stable. Most important of all, you will need to raise your vibrations through unconditional, nonjudgmental love.

"If you have chosen to be beamed aboard a spacecraft, remain calm. Do not panic because fear lowers the frequency of vibrations. While you are in a deep sleep, levitation beams will lift you up to the spacecraft in your physical body. This can occur at any time — the exact date of your liftoff is not yet known. No member of the Spiritual

Hierarchy has yet been authorized to give Earthians a certain date when they will be beamed aboard the mother ships. If a date should be given, use discernment regarding it. What must be stressed is not the moment in time, but the preparation for that moment.

"You will be taken aboard a mother ship where you will be fed, housed, and trained for the work you will be doing. Time will be relative for those of you who will be physically beamed aboard a mother ship. The time spent on the craft before you return to Earth may be only a year or two, while twenty or thirty years may have elapsed on planet Earth. For this reason, provisions have been made to beam families up together. On board you will be trained in advanced technology and other important skills. When it is time for you to be beamed back down to Earth, you will be prepared to take your place as a leader in the new age. As you return to Earth, your physical body will take on great beauty and you will radiate an essence of spiritual light and love.

"The time to uplift some of you in your physical bodies is near at hand. When the liftoff occurs, it will happen fast. You will be beamed up during sleep individually, rather than in groups. We are preparing for all your needs. We are pleased to see this immense task of preparation and planning drawing to a close.

"Before you incarnated, you chose one of these three options as your personal plan. By intuitively being in touch with your Higher Self, you may be able to discover which option you have chosen. Even if you don't yet know exactly what your part in the mission is going to be, don't worry about it. You will be in exactly the right place at the right time to carry out your part in bringing to Earth the Golden Age of Peace."

After the captain had finished speaking to us, he left

the lounge. Then a young female officer with long dark hair, wearing a pale blue jumpsuit, stood up and said, "Those of you who have learned the art of solo astral flight are invited to ask your Higher Self to bring you aboard a mother ship for a visit. We want you to feel that you will always be welcomed. Know this, that we are your brothers and sisters working together with you for the welfare of Earth. We of the Spiritual Hierarchy of this Solar System have combined our own energies to send to your world a mighty outpouring of spiritual love.

"Now before you leave," the officer continued, "I invite you to join me in a toast to our successful mission." Several crew members prepared a table set with beautiful crystal goblets. We had a choice of either pale green, yellow, or pink nectars. As we held our goblets high, the officer said, "Here's to you of Earth. May we work together for universal peace and enlightenment."

It was now time to leave the mother ship, but instead of returning to Earth in a scout craft, we gathered in the transport room. Then, much as on *Star Trek*, our astral bodies were beamed back down to our waiting physical bodies. We brought back with us the knowledge that all is in readiness for those who will call this spaceship home.

After the students had quietly adjusted to being back in their physical bodies, the first question asked was, "How can we know if we have volunteered to be on board a spacecraft?"

"If you have experienced several of the following," I answered, "you may have chosen to be beamed aboard a spaceship: if you have seen a spacecraft or experienced missing time; if you awakened with unexplained wounds or scars; if you have ever experienced an odd displacement in which you found yourself in a different location from the one you'd been in only seconds before; or if you have had recurring dreams about UFOs or space people."

Florence shared with the class: "I have two young children and I was concerned about what would happen to them if I should be beamed aboard a spacecraft. I asked my guide, and she told me that families will be beamed aboard as a group. Then she showed me the school and playground that have been prepared to take care of the needs of the children. I was really impressed with the facility. The ceiling over the play area is very high, rounded, and lighted in such a way that it gives the appearance of sky."

Melanie told the class, "I asked my guide where and how they washed their clothes. I was really amazed when she told me that they are cleaned with ultrasound, which she says works much better than using soap and water. My guide showed me how the clothes are hung in a cabinet and moved along a type of conveyor belt. In about three minutes, they come out at the other end of the cabinet clean and like new."

Jim was one of the last to share his experience with the class, "I guess I've misjudged the aliens. At least the ones I met tonight really seem concerned about our welfare. So I guess that besides the aliens who are portrayed in the movies and on TV as vicious and evil, there are some who really care about the people of Earth. I'm really glad I had the opportunity to meet these space people tonight."

10

Encounters with Angels

Some of the most important and influential inhabitants of the higher astral and celestial worlds are the angelic beings. Angels influence and help us whether we are aware of them or not. When we face personal problems or a tragedy, we should remember that angels are always ready to lend their assistance, comfort, and counsel. In times of accident or emergency, people have experienced the physical protection and help of these angelic beings. Perhaps the stranger who seemed to appear out of nowhere and gave assistance when no other help was available was your own Guardian Angel.

Angels possess natural preferences which permit them to develop along the lines most suited to their temperaments. They work at their tasks with creative joy and a keen sense of selfless service. They are free of negative, human feelings such as impatience, fatigue, or boredom. Usually, when angels assume their duties, they work tirelessly until they have completed their tasks. Every phase of their work is carried out with thoroughness and no detail is slighted.

Through the ages, belief in angels has been a universal theme. Winged figures appear in ancient Sumerian carvings, in Egyptian tombs, and on Assyrian reliefs. The Hittites and Canaanites believed in supernatural messengers. Buddhism and Hinduism recognize the existence of angels. Christians, Jews, and Muslims also believe in their existence. The word "angel" comes from the Latin word *angelus* and the Greek word *angelos*, meaning "messenger." In both the Jewish and Christian religions, angels are considered God's messengers.

Many parallels to Old Testament stories of angels are to be found in ancient, Eastern literature. Angels appear in more than half the books of the Bible. It was an angel who told Abraham to spare his son from sacrifice. Angels saved Daniel from the lion's den, announced to Mary that she was to give birth to a son, and rolled the stone away from Jesus' tomb.

Angels belong to the lowest celestial order. As angels continue to learn and evolve, they take on greater responsibilities until they graduate to the next higher level in the angelic hierarchy. Above the angels are the Archangels. These are not only a rank of angels in the celestial hierarchy; the term is also used to denote all heavenly Beings above the grade of angel. In this sense, "Archangels" could refer to any of the advanced orders of angels. All of these great Beings are androgynous — both male and female.

The Archangels were very much involved with humans in their primal beginnings. Most of these involvements have been deleted from Western literature because of their complex nature. However, some accounts can still be found in the various Eastern texts, in which the Archangels are recognized as having an important part in the many stages of the development of planet Earth.

The first created Beings were perfect because God Almighty, the Prime Creator, could create only perfection. These are the great Archangels or Universal Lords. These great Beings are attuned to the supreme will of God and are God's companions, as they were intended to be.

Since these mighty Archangels possess free will, each manifests in a slightly different way from all the others. They began to experiment with the power of their own creative individuality. Using the blueprint from God Almighty, they created other perfect androgynous beings who became the Solar Lords. These Archangels were given the responsibility of governing the various solar systems.

Later, the Solar Lords took it on themselves to create other Archangels who are the Planetary Lords. These Archangels are responsible for caring for the individual planets in each solar system.

As ages passed, a group of Planetary Lords volunteered to help prepare a new planet, Terra (that is, Earth), for human life. The Planetary Lords were assigned a specific section of Earth as their responsibility. Over eons, they seeded the land with a variety of grasses, plants, bushes, and trees, which they brought with them from their home planets. As the growing things flourished, the Archangels looked at their handiwork and were pleased to see that Terra had been transformed into a beautiful garden. Then the Planetary Lords brought to Terra an assortment of fish, reptiles, birds, insects, and mammals. Some of these were unable to adjust to the environment, but others multiplied.

Finally these Planetary Lords knew that it was time to create human life. Ancient writings relate that the Archangels, using the blueprint of God Almighty, created mankind in their own images, with their own colors of hair, eyes, and skin, and with their own particular body and facial traits. They then passed on to these humans a part of their God essence — a Soul. Thus were humans created. These Archangels are still very much involved with Earth and her inhabitants.

Occasionally angels find it necessary to give help in a concrete way, and they materialize in a physical body for a time. In order to do this, they must slow down their vibrational frequencies to enable them to become visible in the heavier atmosphere of Earth.

It is not surprising that some people who believe that they have had an encounter with an angel are reluctant to discuss it. Very often, the recognition that it was an angelic encounter comes only in retrospect. One of the most exciting experiences involving an angelic intervention was told to me by an elderly man who came up after a lecture I had given on psychic phenomena. This is his story:

> *"For all of these years, I have not told of my experience for fear of being laughed at or considered crazy. But now, I feel that I can speak to you, and you will understand.*
>
> *"It happened during the second world war. My wife and child had left our home in Germany and traveled by train to Switzerland, where I was to meet them as soon as I had taken care of some business, but I waited too long and found myself in a concentration camp; my only crime was that I was a Jew. We were held in a small halfway camp waiting for transportation to one of the larger camps. When word came that we were to be moved the next day, I knew that if I didn't try to escape that night I would probably never*

have another chance. We were close to the Swiss border; however, to get there it would be necessary to go over a high mountain range. I had for many days been thinking of my escape and had carefully saved a small amount of food from my daily ration.

"It was a moonless night as I crawled to the fence and made my way under a loose wire. I walked all that night, only resting long enough to drink from an icy stream and eat a bit of dry bread. I continued walking all the next day, not daring to rest for fear they were searching for me with dogs. By the end of the second night, with no rest and no food, I made a terrible discovery. I had been going around in circles. There was no doubt that those were my tracks in the snow. I was completely discouraged and all hope left me. I had escaped the camp only to die in the bitter cold on this mountainside.

"Just then, I looked up in surprise to see a man coming toward me. He asked where I was headed and I told him the name of the Swiss town where my family was waiting for me. The man told me that he too was going there, and we could walk along together. A feeling of renewed strength filled my body as he shared some of his food with me. Together we walked along the trail that led through the narrow pass in the mountains that I had been trying in vain to find.

"Later, as I stood looking down at the Swiss village far below me, happiness filled my heart. I knew I could never have found my way here without the help of the stranger. I turned around to express my thanks, but he was gone. I retraced my

steps for several yards, but nowhere could I see any footprints in the snow except my own. A feeling of warmth spread through me as I realized that he was my Guardian Angel who had led me from certain death in the snow to safety and a new life that eventually would lead me to America."

When we are born into the physical world, we are attended by the tall, exceedingly loving Angels of Birth. They, like all angels, are sustained by an inbreathing of that energy we call "electricity." The Angels of Birth possess an added capacity: they use this electrical force to unite a Soul with its infant physical body. The fetus can be ensouled any time from conception until the moment of birth, but this usually occurs in the third trimester.

Angels of Healing are always ready to help us when we ask for healing. These angels direct healing currents where they are needed. Through the tranquilizing influence of Healing Angels, the atmosphere surrounding hospitals, nursing homes, and other places of suffering is purified of thoughts of depression and pain, and these negative feelings are replaced with vibrations of peace and hope. When someone becomes ill, these angels first ascertain whether a patient is to be healed or released from the body through death. If their investigation reveals that the person's lifespan is not finished, they inspire doctors with the proper diagnosis and the right treatment. In the new age, through telepathy, we will be able to tune into the Healing Angels as easily as we now tune into our favorite television program. These angels will explain to us the cause of our illness and teach us how to heal our bodies and maintain good health. A Healing Angel touched Virginia in a very special way and changed her life:

"The most significant experience I have had with an angel occurred about thirty years ago. For a long time, I had suffered from terrible migraine headaches. The doctor didn't know what caused them and had been unable to find a cure. He had frightened my mother by telling her that some day I might possibly go into a coma and pass on. I was so miserable that for days I would go around with my hand over my eyes to keep the light out.

"This particular night, I was experiencing an excruciating headache. It was so bad that I was literally staggering around. 'Can't I help you?' my worried mother asked. 'Isn't there something I can do for you?'

"'Mother, just go to bed,' I moaned. 'Leave me alone. There's nothing you can do. Only God can help me now.'

"As I was walking the floor, I thought, I'll take some sleeping pills. It might at least ease the pain a bit. I went into the bathroom in the dark because I couldn't stand the light. When I reached up to get the sleeping pills, I was suddenly encircled with a light so bright that everything in the room faded from my sight. I felt as if I were standing in space with a breeze blowing around me. The first thing that entered my mind was, My God, I've died. This is the moment; this is the time. Oh, my poor mother. She has a bad heart and she's going to walk into the bathroom and find my body on the floor and she'll probably have a heart attack.

"While the bright light completely surrounded me and a breeze softly caressed me, I saw in

my mind's eye a tall figure of an angel. He was dressed in a long brown robe with the cowl thrown back and a rope tied around his waist. He said these words, which I will never forget, 'Fear not, little one, for I am here to help you.' He raised his hand and put it on my forehead. I felt every finger as he slowly passed his hand up and down my head to the base of my skull. As he did this, all my pain vanished. 'I must go now,' he said. 'I bless you.'

"Then the light was gone and everything came back into focus. I stood there amazed. There was no pain — not even an after pain. I felt wonderful. When I switched on the bathroom light and looked directly at it, there was no pain. I dashed into my mother's bedroom, turned on the light and cried excitedly, 'Look, mother. Look! My pain is gone.'

"She couldn't believe it and remarked, 'My poor daughter, what's happened? Have you lost your mind?'

"'Look, Mother,' I replied. 'Remember before I couldn't even stoop down? Now watch this,' and I put my head between my knees. 'I can look into the light and roll my head around and no pain!' Then I told her about my amazing experience.

"'I would never have believed it,' murmured my mother, 'if I hadn't been here to witness what has happened with my own eyes. Before, when your migraine had gone, your head would be sore and tender for days and you couldn't move your head without pain. Virginia, I do believe you're healed.'

"She was right. The migraines have never recurred."

In my classes on spiritual healing, I teach a very simple yet effective method of healing that you might find useful. First, ask to be healed. You don't have to specify what the illness is because your Guardian Angel, your Higher Self, already knows. Second, receive the healing energy that comes from God, through your Higher Self. In an altered state, with your eyes closed, visualize the energy coming into your crown center at the top of your head and flowing through you, bringing peace, relaxation, and healing to every cell of your body. You may even feel a tingling in your hands and feet as the energy flows through your body. When the healing energy stops flowing, sit quietly for a few minutes. Third, give thanks to your Higher Self for the healing. I suggest that you set aside a certain time each day to receive this healing.

Each chapel, temple, and great cathedral contains an Angel of Adoration. When the church is filled with worshipers, the number of angels is increased according to the spiritual love of the congregation. Sadly, some religions have let their spiritual flame go out. They have become so entangled in manmade rules and regulations that they have forgotten that the spiritual path is the way of unconditional love. In these places of worship, the Angels of Adoration wait patiently for the leaders and the members of the congregation to rekindle their spiritual flame of love.

One Sunday morning my daughter and I were sitting near the front of our large church in the San Fernando Valley. While the choir sang the anthem, I closed my eyes to better enjoy the inspiring music. As the choir continued singing, the minister began his sermon. I opened my eyes to see why this strange event was happening. The choir members were sitting quietly in their seats, but standing behind them was an angelic choir still sharing their song with those in the congregation who were able to tune in to their heavenly music. When the celestial choirs sing, it is from their hearts, and although most of us may not be consciously aware of their music, there springs up within us a surging and enlivening of our higher states of consciousness.

Angels of Prayer are also present in places of worship. They not only uplift the consciousness of the congregation but are also concerned with the prayers of individual members. Prayer is a powerful force, and when a group of people earnestly pray for the same thing, it multiplies that power even more. The words that are used in prayer are not as important as the sincerity of the heart.

Prayer is conversation with God, our God Self. It is not necessary for us to be in a house of worship to have our prayers answered. We can pray any time and anywhere. If we are praying for the healing or protection of somcone else, our Higher Self directs our thoughts to the Guardian Angel of that person. If the prayer is for ourselves, it is answered by our Higher Self. Sometimes the answer is "yes," sometimes "no," sometimes "not at this time," but always our prayers are answered personally with great wisdom and love.

When the time comes for us to leave this physical plane and cross the threshold into the next world, the Angel of Death stands by our side. This angel fills the human soul with confidence and a willingness to go forward into the next dimension of existence. The Angels of Death are compassionate and gentle and usually appear as feminine. However, in the inspiring television program, *Touched by an Angel*, John Dye beautifully portrays the Angel of Death as a handsome, caring young man.

The following encounter with an Angel of Death was told to me by a woman who did not wish to have her name included:

> *"Back in the mid-1950s, when I was working for a hospital in Redwood City, California, a being I will call the 'Angel of Death' walked through my room. It happened one night while I was living in the nurse's quarters, although I was a secretary and not a nurse. Because of a problem we had been having with the night watchman, I had made especially sure that my door was locked and bolted. Even though I was lying on my bed reading, I was still wearing slacks and a sweater because I planned to go downstairs and have some coffee with a friend when she got off duty around midnight.*
>
> *"Because I smoke in bed, I'm always careful, so when I saw a puff of white off to my right, I turned my head to make sure it was not smoke building up in my room. But it wasn't smoke. It was a lovely girl about sixteen years of age, wearing a white Grecian-style dress which hung in three tiers of pleats. She had beautiful golden hair falling down over her shoulders. Her skin was pure white and she had exquisite features and pale blue eyes. I was surprised to see that she was barefoot. As she walked across the room toward the wall facing the outside of the building, she put her finger to her lips as if to shush me and keep me from speaking.*
>
> *"My mind took all this calmly and I was*

thinking, 'My, now who could this girl be and how did she get into my locked room?' Although my mind was calm, my body reacted like you wouldn't believe. Every bone in my body seemed to be vibrating so violently that I did not think I would even be able to collect myself enough to get out of bed. My heart pounded as shock waves went up and down my body. All the while, I was thinking how silly I must look and how impolite I was being to such a lovely person who certainly had done nothing at all to frighten me. Just then she walked through the wall and disappeared. The moment she was gone, my body stopped reacting and sleep overpowered me. All I had time to do was make sure my cigarette was out. I set the ashtray aside and fell back upon my pillow sound asleep.

"The next day I awakened feeling fine. When I went to the cafeteria for breakfast, I saw my favorite nurse looking pensive. As we ate together, she told me that one of her patients, a man, had died in the night. Few people ever died in that hospital because it was for respiratory diseases and most people were cured and released. In fact, there were seldom more than one or two deaths a year.

"The nurse told me that this man was the kind of patient who would never make demands or impose on the nurses in any way. He would get up himself rather than call a nurse. I could tell that my friend was deeply moved by the patient's death. When I told her of the vision I had seen the night before, she said that it must have been the Angel of Death, because the man had died about

the same time that the angel had walked through my locked room."

Sometimes we may be called upon to help an Angel of Death. The following story, by Virginia Seely, demonstrates the love and concern of an angel for her young charge:

"My husband was away on a business trip so I decided to stay overnight with my sister. We lay in bed talking for awhile before turning off the light. When we finally said good night, I closed my eyes and relaxed completely. Then, to my surprise, I found myself out of my physical body and standing by the bed in my spirit body. There in my arms was a little boy of three or four dressed in a white hospital gown.

"'Please don't let them take me,' he whimpered. 'I don't want to be hurt any more. I don't want to be hurt.'

"'Don't worry,' I assured him, 'Nobody is going to hurt you. I'll take care of you, so don't worry.' I looked up and saw an angelic being in a long, white robe standing in the doorway. Through mental telepathy, I was informed that this little boy had been sick all of his life. Time and time again he had been in hospitals and operating rooms, and he was very frightened. When he died, the angel didn't want to frighten him further or take him under protest, so she was using me as a channel to calm him.

"'Look,' I said to the little boy. 'An angel has come to take you to a beautiful place where you'll never suffer again. She is taking you away from

all the pain.'

"The angel just stood there gazing lovingly at him. 'Promise you won't let her hurt me,' he whispered.

"'She won't hurt you,' I replied. 'She is here to help you. Now it is time for you to go with her.' The little boy held out his arms to the angel, who lovingly gathered him to her breast. As he cuddled up to her, the vision faded from my sight."

The most important angel to us is our own Guardian Angel, who has been a part of our life since the beginning. Many names have been used in referring to our Guardian Angel: Twin Soul, Higher Self, Oversoul, Holy Spirit, God Self. It really doesn't matter what name we use as long as we realize that it is actually a part of our own being. Our Guardian Angel plays many roles in our life: Celestial Mother, Protector, Teacher, Guide, Comforter, and Spiritual Partner.

When we are children, our Guardian Angel has the role of Celestial Mother. There is an extremely close relationship between most children and their Guardian Angels. Not only do children communicate with their angels during sleep; some are able to see and converse with them during their waking hours. At times, an angel may take on a physical form to be a playmate, companion, and protector to the child. If you have a child who sees or talks to his special angel, be careful that you don't discount the validity of your child's experience. What the child believes is *true* is indeed truth for him.

Sometimes angels may even take on the form of an animal in order to have a more personal relationship with the children in their care. My friend June Austin tells of her childhood playmate:

"From a very early age until I was four, my angel was with me in the form of a small koala bear. He was invisible to mom and dad, so they thought he was an imaginary playmate, but he was my very real friend and confidant. During those years, we lived near a wooded area where my little koala and I would play hide and seek, tag, and follow the leader until we were exhausted. At night, I would tuck him into bed in a place I made for him beside our woodstove; however, he would never stay there for long. After Mom and Dad were asleep, he would sneak into my room where we would giggle and talk for hours.

"As time passed and I was almost old enough for school, I sensed that my little friend would soon be leaving me. It made me feel sad and lonely. Just before he left, he told me who he really was — not a furry little koala, but my very own angel who would never be more than a thought away."

No matter what age we are, there may be a time when we feel lonely, depressed, or ill. How comforting it is to intuitively feel the loving presence of our Guardian Angel holding our hand and reminding us that we are never alone. If you find it difficult to visualize your Guardian Angel, picture in your mind the most loving, caring person in your life. The mind is more powerful than we realize, and it is possible for a Guardian Angel to merge with this thought form and bring us the comfort and healing that we need.

If we find ourselves in a threatening situation, our Guardian Angel takes on the role of protector. We can visualize a knight in shining armor standing by our side and protecting us with his shield. Another form of protection is the White Light that is an essence of our Higher Self, our Guardian Angel. We can ask that the White Light surround and protect us and our loved ones. When we travel, it is wise to visualize the White Light surrounding the whole car, bus, train, or airplane, protecting everyone on board.

As a partner, our Guardian Angel is interested not only in the spiritual part of our life but also in our career, marriage, and family. Either orally or silently, we can communicate with our Guardian Angel just as we would talk to our closest and wisest friend. Our Celestial Partner knows all our needs but usually does not lend assistance until we ask for help and guidance.

When we begin to mature spiritually and are consciously seeking to understand the purpose for our life, our Guardian Angel becomes our teacher and exerts a great influence over our progress and destiny. Our Guardian Angel will not intrude upon our personal free will or make choices for us, but can surround us with new interests and direct new stimuli into our life. Through the direction of our Guardian Angel, we may be led to various teachers who will help us in our spiritual growth, but we don't have to search far and wide for a special guru or master, because our Guardian Angel is our own personal spiritual teacher.

As we become aware of our spiritual heritage, we will also become consciously aware of the Guardian Angel's role as Indwelling Master, who is of the greatest importance to our higher spiritual progress. When we align ourselves in love and thought with our Guardian Angel, we will experience her guidance and protection in all our endeavors. We will also begin to realize that we are one with our Guardian Angel — that we are indeed Twin Souls.

Angels sometimes appear suddenly during times of great danger. Their bright and beautiful appearance may cause fear and awe. When their work is finished, the common experience is to see them vanish instantly. A. C. Ferber first printed his father's encounter with an angel in his book *We Are Immortal*. He has given me permission to reprint it:

> *"My father was fond of relating the following event to his immediate family because it was the most remarkable experience of his entire life. When he was a young man, my father learned the carpenter's trade. One day, as he was helping to tear down an old building, the floor above him suddenly collapsed. Timbers and debris came crashing down all around him. He thought that his last moment on Earth had come. 'Just then,' he related, 'I saw an angel in front of me, in the middle of all that dust and wreckage.'*
>
> *"By some miracle, my father came out of that experience not only alive, but unhurt. Because of the angel's intervention, the framework of the building fell in such a way that it blocked the path of debris which might otherwise have killed him. He suffered only a temporary annoyance from the inhalation of dust.*
>
> *"Later, when I asked my father how he knew it was an angel, he replied impatiently, 'Because he had wings!' From my research, I have discovered that angels do not have wings. However, I believe that when an angel appears to someone here on Earth, he usually appears in the form that*

the individual thinks he will have. In other words, since my father thought angels have wings, the angel appeared with wings."

Many early artists drew angels without wings. More recent artists, however, usually represent them with wings. The vibrant energy which surrounds the angels might easily be interpreted as wings. Angels, however, do not need wings to move from place to place but travel with the speed of thought.

Angels are on a different life stream than humans. We do not become angels when we die, and an angel seldom if ever takes on a physical body for a whole lifetime. God's universe is not stagnant. All have the opportunity to evolve. Angels and humans alike experience many initiations as they progress along their particular life paths.

Our Guardian Angel's role is one of healer, protector, comforter, and teacher. At birth, at marriage, and at death, as well as at other significant times, we are attended by angels, and they exert a great influence in our lives. Nearly every field of human endeavor receives mental and inspirational stimulus from angels. They do not seek or want our homage but desire only our love, trust, and respectful cooperation. Truly, God does give His angels charge over us to keep us in all our ways.

11

Exploring the Higher Astral Realms

After all the students had spread out their sleeping bags, I said to the class, "Because tonight is our last time to meet together, I have planned something very special for us. While we are exploring the higher astral planes, some of you will be invited to take part in an initiation. In the days of Atlantis and later in ancient Egypt, Greece, and other evolved countries, initiations were conducted in the temples of Earth. But as time passed, more of the initiations began to take place only in the higher realms. Finally they ceased to be conducted on the physical plane. An initiation can be compared to receiving a diploma when you graduate. There is a series of initiations, each denoting a step upward in your spiritual journey. You have probably taken part in one or more astral initiations, although your conscious mind may not be aware of the experience. Because you are able to travel astrally, it is now possible for you to be aware of your spiritual achievements and take part in an initiation in the higher realms.

"The Higher Self is the one who determines when the student is ready to participate in an initiation. Tonight some of you will be intuitively told that you are ready. The other members of our class will be a part of the audience.

Those of you who feel that you are ready may mentally send to your friends and loved ones an invitation to attend this spiritual celebration. Your guests may be residing in either the Earth or astral world. They do not need to know how to astral-travel, since they will be brought to the ceremony by their Higher Self." For the next few moments, the students sat in quiet meditation as they intuitively sent out their invitations.

Then I helped the students achieve an altered state of consciousness by saying, "Relax ... relax your body ... relax your mind ... release all tension. As I count from one to twenty, you will enter a deep alpha state. Now I want you to visualize yourself entering the astral elevator. As the elevator doors close, feel yourself moving upward to the higher astral planes."

When the elevator doors open, we can find no words to describe the view that greets our eyes. We are surrounded with joy, love, and peace beyond earthly comprehension. The air is filled with the celestial music of harps, flutes, and angelic voices. Both my students and I search for words to describe the ethereal beauty of these higher realms.

The buildings and homes are flawless. We observe that some of the buildings appear to be made of alabaster and that they glow with an inner light. Some of the structures are made of a very refined crystalline substance which looks like sunlit glass. Much of the architecture is reminiscent of the splendor of the golden age of ancient Greece. There are long colonnades lined with graceful marble columns and open courtyards where astral citizens gather to share their wisdom and their philosophical views. Sitting on one of the balconies are several white doves, preening and cooing to each other. On the higher planes, all the animals live in harmony with one another.

Many people think of the higher planes of the astral world as Heaven, but the truth is that Heaven can be within each of us right now. We are creating Heaven, or even Hell, every day of our lives by our thoughts and actions. When we are in a heavenly state of consciousness, we have a feeling of inner peace and contentment; we are consciously aware that we are divinely protected and greatly loved; and we know that we are one with our Higher Self, the God essence within each of us. When we understand the truth about Heaven, we can begin creating our own Heaven right here on Earth.

The Buddhist idea of a heavenly place is Nirvana. Here perfect happiness is reached and the Soul is free from all desire, suffering, and karma. Another name for the higher astral planes is "Paradise." Paradise was originally a Persian word used to describe the enclosed pleasure gardens of royalty. The Greeks borrowed the word from the Persians. Later the early Christians used the name to mean the home of the blessed dead. In Greek mythology, the Elysian Fields were where good Souls were sent after death. It was a place of song and sunlight and the air was sweet and cool. Souls lived there among the flowers and meadows, expressing joy and love.

Most religions call the higher realms "Heaven" and believe the Souls of good people go there after death. They picture Heaven as a place where everything is perfect. Desert people imagine Heaven as a pleasant oasis with plenty of water. Some people may believe that the streets are paved with gold and everyone is on a permanent vacation. At first, we will experience the higher astral realm in our own ways, until we are ready to understand that it is a place filled with love and laughter where we can continue to learn and evolve emotionally, mentally, and spiritually.

Those who reside here are highly evolved. Many are ascended Masters who have completed their lives on the physical plane and are no longer required to return to a physical body. These Masters are often referred to as "Spirit Teachers," "Spirit Helpers," or "Spirit Guides." The robes they wear are usually white, but they may be any brilliant or subtle color imaginable. These Masters, both men and women, have melded the best of the masculine and feminine qualities into a perfect whole. Surrounding them is an aura of Godliness, and their eyes reflect great wisdom. Often these evolved astral citizens are mistakenly identified as Jesus or one of the angels.

In the higher realms, occupations are designed to help influence the physical world toward better living standards, brotherly love, and global peace. There is no particular religion here — only pure spiritual love that is unconditional and nonjudgmental.

One of the first places I enjoy taking my class when we visit the higher astral realms is a heavenly garden filled with a fragrance reminiscent of orange blossoms. This tranquil garden is a special place where people of Earth, traveling astrally, are able to meet with friends and loved ones who are on the Other Side.

The students in my classes enjoy visiting this special garden, where they are given an opportunity to meet with their loved ones who have "died" and with their Higher Selves. We usually end our visit to the garden with a beautiful ceremony. We gather around a large fountain where the water cascades down from level to level. Then each student mentally creates a personal goblet: some are composed of crystal, and others are created out of various kinds of precious or semiprecious metals. With their Higher Self standing behind them, embracing them with love, the students fill their goblets with water from the fountain. As they drink this living water, it brings healing and peace to every cell of their bodies. You too are invited to drink from the fountain when you astrally visit this heavenly garden.

As we were standing in the garden, a Master came over to our group and informed us that it was time to prepare for the initiation ceremony. He led the way through the garden to a beautiful cathedral. Words are inadequate to describe this holy place. The large cathedral appeared to be constructed of a crystalline material, while the spire seemed to be composed of giant crystals of varying lengths reaching skyward. As the sunlight shone through the cathedral walls, the reflected rainbow of colors shimmered and sparkled making the whole building appear alive.

The rest of our group entered the cathedral and were seated, while the four initiates were taken to private rooms. There they were bathed, anointed with scented oil, and dressed in robes of their own choosing. When all was in readiness, they were led to the entrance of the cathedral where the ceremony would take place. Celestial music filled the air as the initiates and their Higher Selves, arm in arm, made their way down the center aisle to the altar. As their Higher Self stood behind them, they knelt in preparation for the ceremony. A Master, whose aura shone like the midday sun, stepped up to the altar and spoke to the initiates and to their guests:

> *"Blessings to each of you. We have come together today to recognize your achievement in reaching another milestone in your spiritual pilgrimage. Remember that it is love that will change you and your world. As you grow more loving of yourself and others, you will begin seeing every person as a perfect being, just the way*

they are. Loving yourself will dissolve your ego, and you will feel no need to prove that you are superior to anyone. Then you will treat everyone as equal to yourself.

"The more you love yourself and others, the faster you vibrate. If your world looks beautiful and safe and you feel rich pleasure in every moment, then you are vibrating rapidly. If your world appears gloomy or frightening, then you are vibrating slowly. Indeed, your daily life is an expression of your spiritual life. Your life will change as you become more loving — perhaps, however, not in ways that you can predict. It is important for you to remember that it is really not what happens in your life that is important, it is how you react to what happens. I challenge you, today, always to walk with love. As you go out from this holy place, know that you are surrounded by our eternal love. May God bless each of you."

When the Master had finished speaking, he went to each of the kneeling initiates in turn and placed upon each one's head a crown of righteousness. Then with a crescendo of harps, flutes, and angelic voices, the initiates and their Higher Selves walked back up the aisle and out of the cathedral.

When *you* are spiritually ready to receive an initiation, it will happen. *When the student is ready, the Master appears.* You may not be consciously aware of the initiation, but on the inner planes you will rejoice in your spiritual achievement.

After the initiation ceremony, the students wandered awestruck through the cathedral and gardens, absorbing the tremendous beauty and joy that were evident everywhere. Finally, the students and I made our way to a courtyard which was surrounded by marble pillars. Near the center of this courtyard was a fantastic fountain composed of water, light, and sound. Here we joined a group of people who had gathered to hear a discourse by one of the Masters:

> *"No matter how wonderful or beautiful these higher planes appear to you, they are not your true home. Remember the old saying, 'Home is where the heart is'? Well, home is where your beloved Higher Self, your Twin Soul, dwells. Your Twin Soul may dwell in the fifth dimension of Earth or even on another planet.*
>
> *"You will remain in the third dimension as long as there are lessons to learn and work to complete. When you arrive in the next dimension, you will be attracted to exactly the right place where you can continue your education. The more highly evolved you are, the less time you will need to spend in the next dimension. Then, once again, you will go through the process called 'death.' This time you will leave behind your astral body and take up residence in your Soul body. This is your true self ... your Eternal Self.*
>
> *"The fifth dimension, which some call the Celestial Realms, allows no negativity within its borders. Because you are probably not yet perfect, it is necessary for you to leave behind any negativity that you may have brought with you. Let me explain this by using Earth terminology. Outside the gates of the fifth dimension is a large*

waiting room. There are many lockers here with a name on each locker. You are to put all of your negativity into your locker, where it will remain until you are ready to return to another physical life.

"For those who are not spiritually evolved, the time spent in the fifth dimension is like being in a deep sleep. They are unaware of their Higher Self's arms around them. They cannot appreciate the beauty, peace, and love that surround them. You who are more highly evolved will be eager and excited to leave the astral planes and enter the Celestial Realms, where you will be greeted by your Higher Self. What joy and bliss you will feel as your Twin Soul embraces you! You will know that, once again, you have come home."

As the Master finished speaking, I realized that it was time to leave these higher realms. We had been traveling astrally for a little over an hour, and, as much as we would have enjoyed lingering in this peaceful environment, it was time to return to our physical bodies. We entered the astral elevator and in a short while we were back in our classroom. I reminded the students, "You will be able to remember everything you saw, heard, and experienced. It will be clear in your mind. Now, I'm going to count backwards from three to one, and when I reach one you will once again be in your physical body. Three … awake, alert, and aware. Two … awake, alert, and aware. One … awake, alert, and aware. When you are ready, you may open your eyes."

For a long time the students sat silently almost as if they were mesmerized. No one moved or talked for a long time until they were finally ready to share their experience with the others. The four initiates were especially quiet, and they seemed reluctant to share their private thoughts with anyone else. They each agreed that this initiation would change their lives forever.

After everyone had shared their astral experiences, I asked if anyone had a question. A young woman spoke up, "Several times I heard the Master refer to our Twin Soul. What is the difference between a soul mate and a Twin Soul?"

"That is a good question, since there are those who have confused the terms 'soul mate' and 'Twin Soul.' A soul mate is someone we have been with in many lifetimes: as a parent and child, as siblings, as husband and wife, or as close friends both in the third and fourth dimension. Usually the bond of love becomes stronger and more intense with each incarnation. Sometimes our soul mate is the same sex as we are. In one lifetime we may not find a soul mate, while in another lifetime we may meet several soul mates.

"Our Twin Soul does not incarnate on the physical or astral planes but dwells in the higher dimensions and has been with us since the beginning of time. Other names for the Twin Soul are Twin Flames, Higher Self, Holy Spirit, God Self, and Guardian Angel. It matters not what name we use, as long as we remember that we are one with our Twin Soul."

The students and I had shared a wonderful adventure together and we were reluctant to part, but the hour was late, so the students rolled up their sleeping bags and drove off into the night.

12

The New World of the 21st Century

Earth is changing in profound ways as a new consciousness is being born. As we move into the 21st century, we need to trust that all is unfolding according to the great cosmic plan for Earth's transformation. In the days of Atlantis, Earth was preparing to make the quantum leap from the third to the fourth dimension. But the people of that time were more involved with the material and were neglecting their spiritual path. The citizens of that thriving country failed to raise their vibrations through love, and a great civilization fell into the sea. Destruction has come to every civilization that has chosen to allow negative vibrations to flourish.

Once again we are preparing for this tremendous opportunity to take our rightful place among the planets of our solar system. Earth is the laggard. We are the last planet in this solar system that is still third-dimensional. Earth is preparing to be transformed into a fourth-dimensional planet. Some have called this the end of the world. In a way, it will be the end of Earth as we know it. When the transformation is completed, the negativity that has engulfed our planet for ages will be cleansed from Earth. While it is true that we are all spiritual beings, some have forgotten their divinity and have chosen not to raise their vibrations with love. These people will no longer be allowed to incarnate on Earth but will be sent to another planet where they can continue to work toward spiritual enlightenment.

Earth changes have been occurring throughout the billions of years of our planet's history. However, these changes are now being accelerated. According to many prophecies, there will be an increase in natural catastrophes as we near the end of this age. Between now and the year 2012, there will be more and more earthquakes, volcanic eruptions, tidal waves, and other natural disasters. There will be a tremendous loss of life and many injuries which will change the lives of hundreds of thousands of people. This is all part of the cosmic plan for the transformation of planet Earth and her inhabitants. Remember that we are immortal, spiritual Beings. We do not die. We merely change our consciousness from our physical body to a higher body.

We may wonder why Earth needs to become fourth-dimensional. Now is the time for our third-dimensional, dualistic world to be brought into balance. In the higher dimensions, the polarities of good and evil, right and wrong, do not exist as we know them. When Earth is transformed, she will no longer be surrounded by the negativity she has endured for countless ages. Then the lower planes of the astral world will no longer be needed and they will cease to exist. The astral citizens who dwell in these lower planes will be transported to another planet where they will again be given the opportunity to learn the lessons of love.

There are those who claim that our solar system is preparing to enter a vast region called the Photon Belt. It is said that this Photon Belt is a huge mass of light and highly charged energy. This light and energy has the power to transform our whole solar system. When this profound event occurs, planet Earth will have the impetus to change from its third dimensional density to the fourth dimension.

The actual time when our solar system will enter the Photon Belt cannot be pinpointed, since there are too many variables involved. When this event occurs, some believe that there will be three days of darkness. The cause of this darkness might be from a series of volcanic eruptions which would send so much debris into the atmosphere that it would block out the Sun. It is possible that the darkness might be caused by a comet hitting the Earth. A few years ago, the idea of the Earth being hit by a comet or an asteroid was not taken seriously. However, in July 1994 we saw the incredible explosion as a comet struck Jupiter at a velocity of 140,000 miles per hour. This persuaded doubters that there is indeed a reason to be concerned. Scientists believe that once every 100,000 years a large comet or asteroid hits the Earth. Something that huge would cause global destruction. The force of the impact would generate enormous heat. Millions of tons of rocky debris and dust would billow upward in a gigantic cloud, causing darkness that could last as long as six months. If some morning we wake up and there is only darkness, we need to remain calm. It has been suggested that we stay near or in our homes during this period of darkness, because this event will probably produce mass hysteria among those who are unaware. We need to remain calm and reassure others that this is a part of the cosmic plan for Earth.

Now is the time for us to prepare ourselves by raising our vibrations through spiritual love so that we will be ready for Earth's transformation. We are very much like a violin. Each string of the violin vibrates at a different frequency. If a violin string is not tuned properly, the sound will be discordant. It takes fine tuning of all the strings to make beautiful music. We have four bodies which also vibrate on different frequencies. If even one of these bodies is not properly tuned, we will not be able to experience the full potential harmony of our life.

Each of our bodies is important to the whole person. The physical body is the one we use in the physical world. The energy body is about an inch larger and is the power source for the physical body. The emotional (astral) body is the vehicle we use in the astral world. It is about six inches larger and it interpenetrates both the energy and physical body. The soul body, containing the God essence, surrounds and interpenetrates every cell of our emotional, energy, and physical bodies. The more spiritual (loving) we are, the larger our soul body becomes and the more it glows with an inner radiance. The soul body is our eternal body, the one we use in the higher realms. It is imperative that we "fine tune" our physical, energy, emotional, and soul bodies and bring them into perfect harmony so we will be prepared for the higher energies of the new world.

The process of transforming our bodies from the vibrations of the third dimension to those of the fourth is being accelerated at a tremendous pace so that we will be prepared to handle the incoming energies. As the electromagnetic energy is increased and we absorb these transforming rays, we will feel their effect more and more. It is important that we recognize and learn to adapt to the changes that are taking place within our bodies. We are used to physical activity making us tired, but now internal activity, of which we may not be aware, can also make us exhausted. This tiredness is a signal that we need more rest because of the changes that are occurring within our body. Our blood pressure and body temperature may become lower than what is considered normal. We may also notice that the aging process, which seems to be happening quite rapidly to some people, will start to slow down and become stabilized.

We are straddling two dimensions. We are living in a third-dimensional world, while our bodies are adjusting to the fourth dimension. As we learn to control our emotions and bring our bodies into harmony and alignment, not only will we begin to operate in the fourth dimension — but we will also have the capability of experiencing the fifth dimension.

We should be excited about what is happening to our planet and not fear the future. It is certainly wise to be prepared for Earth's transformation, but we do not need to fear these impending changes. Fear can be a big challenge, for it prevents us from living in a state of peace and joy. Fear involves something that might happen, but that hasn't happened yet. Since fear belongs to the realm of the mind and not the Soul, we can overcome it by changing our thoughts and perceptions. We can replace fear with faith, then we will have the strength to cope with whatever happens to us in the future. Faith is the power that frees us from worry, anxiety, and fear of the unknown. We do not need to search for a safe place where we can escape the changes which may occur on Earth. Instead, we need to have faith that, with the help of our Higher Self, we will be in exactly the right place to carry out our mission in the 21st century.

The time of Earth's transformation is near. It is already being felt on physical, emotional, and spiritual levels. When Earth makes the quantum leap into the fourth dimension, the cells and atoms in every plant, animal, and human will be affected. We may not understand all of the changes that are occurring, but we can trust that what we truly need to know will be revealed to us. In this way, we can experience an inner peace and centeredness.

Before we incarnated, we made some very important decisions concerning the role that we are to play in helping Earth achieve her goal of ascending into the fourth dimension. We chose our parents and the environment we would be born into. We also chose certain lessons to learn and certain karmic debts to repay. We attracted to ourselves everything we needed in the way of experiences, resources, and people to help us learn these lessons and repay our karmic debts. Every moment of our lives we are creating our future. Every decision we make sets us in a definite direction. There may be times when we find ourselves dealing with doubts, fears, and depression. When this occurs, we need to remind ourselves who we really are and why we are here. We need to discover our personal place in the great scheme of things.

Many of us have volunteered to be a part of the action in this important time in Earth's history. Some have come from distant places in the universe to help Earth give birth to the New Age. Some of us have walked among the Earthians and identified closely with them without realizing that we are not of Earth. We've worked, sacrificed, and endured. Now we are ready to wake up and understand our divine mission.

Whether we are aware of it or not, each of us has a plan for this time of transformation. Some will be survivors who will remain on Earth. They will need to be strong and full of courage to help those who are fearful or confused. Others have chosen to be physically beamed aboard a spacecraft where they will be given special training. After Earth has gone through an adjustment period, those who volunteered to be beamed aboard a space station will be returned to Earth in their physical body. They will bring with them all the skills and knowledge that they gained to prepare them to be leaders in the new world.

Some have chosen to leave Earth through death and continue their education in the astral world. When they have finished their training in the universities on the astral planes, they will be eager to bring that information back to Earth and take their place as leaders in the new age.

Rather than being born into a physical body, some may choose to enter the physical plane through a Soul exchange, which has also been referred to as "being a walk-in." Sometimes at death, we leave behind a physical body that is in fairly good condition. Just as many people are now willing to donate parts of their bodies at death to help give life to others, there are some who agree to allow the physical body to be used by an incarnating Soul. The Higher Self of the person who is leaving her physical body through death, and the Higher Self of the person who wishes to incarnate into an adult body, must both approve of the plan. These two people need to be similar in vibration, just as in an organ transplant there must be compatibility between the donor and the recipient.

The criteria for judging whether a Soul exchange has occurred usually include a time of unconsciousness, either as the result of an accident or illness, and, to a lesser or greater degree, a change of personality and spiritual beliefs. Often the person is confused because she may not yet be aware of what has happened to her. Sometimes there is a change in the physical body, including health and food preferences. The departing Soul leaves a copy of the memory of her life; otherwise, the incoming Soul would experience a form of amnesia.

One advantage of a Soul exchange is that it makes it easier to consciously bring into the physical plane cosmic wisdom and understanding, which are often forgotten during the usual birth process. It is also possible to bypass the sometimes tedious experiences of childhood. Another advantage is that at this time in Earth's history there is an urgent need to have more Light Workers out in the field helping to bring forth the Age of Peace. Adults are needed now.

There are disadvantages, too. Some who experience a Soul exchange find it difficult to adjust to the physical world. They may even feel that they are experiencing a nervous breakdown. Some become extremely homesick for their partner — their Higher Self. I speak not only from personal experience but also from having counseled people who have experienced a Soul exchange.

In the 21st century we will see tremendous advances in both science and medicine as the Masters in the higher dimensions continue to communicate their discoveries telepathically to doctors and scientists on Earth. Little by little, the invisible world is becoming visible. Most cells, which are the basic unit of all living things, are invisible except under a microscope. Through the microscope, we are able to see a miniature world in a drop of water. The microscope reveals an entire universe of organisms too small to be seen by the unaided eye.

As more powerful telescopes are built, astronomers are discovering more of the mysteries of the universe and finding stars which are invisible to the human eye. Since the Hubbell Space Telescope was launched, astronomers have been able to observe the birth and death of distant stars. Now the search is on to find planets that support life as we know it.

We have taken some giant steps forward in making visible that which, up to this time, had been invisible. Now we are on the verge of making a quantum leap which will reveal all of the unseen world in our midst as planet Earth and her inhabitants move into the fourth dimension.

We are a unique civilization. Earth does not have just one race, just one spiritual belief. We are a mixture of many races and religions. There is not just one religion, philosophy, or group of people who are endowed with all of the answers. All of us are free to follow the spiritual path that we have chosen and to find our own Truth. We should be careful that we do not judge or criticize others for the paths that they have chosen or for their understanding of truth. Even though we may be on a different level of awareness, no person is better than another.

In the 21st century, we will see a gradual change in our religious beliefs. Many of the religious doctrines were fashioned by medieval priests in order to keep the people in bondage to the church. Although true spirituality may be present in many forms, people have become more and more burdened with manmade rules and regulations. The time has come for all religions to let go of what is obsolete and to unite in love. The new religion will be the spiritual path of unconditional, nonjudgmental love.

Many different religions are waiting for their particular Masters to return at the beginning of this new age. The Jews are expecting their Messiah. The Christians are looking forward to the second coming of Jesus the Christ. Buddhists expect the return of Maitreya Buddha. The Hindus expect the avatar of the new age. Many believe that the World Teacher will come at the beginning of the 21st century. The truth is that all of these religions will realize their hopes and dreams. Not just a single Master will return to Earth: instead, many will cooperate as World Teachers who will help us to create the Age of Peace on planet Earth.

Some believe that the headquarters for these Masters will be in a huge spaceship that will be in orbit above the

Earth. In the last book of the Bible, John gives a wonderful description of Earth's world capital:

> *"I watched that wondrous city, the holy Jerusalem, descending out of the skies from God. It was filled with the glory of God and glowed like a precious gem. The angel held in his hand a golden measuring stick to measure the city. When he measured it, he found it was in the form of a cube, for its height was exactly the same as its other dimensions ... 1,500 miles each way. Its light will light the nations of the Earth, and the rulers of the world will come and bring their glory to it."* (Rev. 21:10, 15, 16, 24)

Certainly, the only way the new Jerusalem could be in the form of a cube would be if it is a giant spaceship stationed above the Earth. All religions will look to the new Jerusalem as their spiritual headquarters, and they will seek spiritual guidance of their own Master. All religions will finally be united in love. Nothing has the power to stand in the way of love, because love is the most powerful force in the whole universe.

The time has come for us truly to realize that we are eternal beings. Although our lives here on Earth last for only a comparatively short while, yet time before and time after are unlimited. Some of us may spend our whole physical life absorbed in our everyday business and ignore this truth. When we finally understand infinity, our concepts of finite time and space will be changed forever. Our personal problems, as well as global problems, will not seem that important when seen in the light of eternity. In the near future, we will find ourselves abandoning the nonessential parts of our lives as we prepare for the great cosmic adventure that awaits us in the 21st century.

As Earth is transformed into a fourth-dimensional planet, our world will be cleansed. We will no longer be burdened by the negativity of the lower astral planes. We will no longer have to contend with the hatred and treachery of the Renegades. Only qualified Souls will be allowed to incarnate upon our planet — only those who have raised their vibrations through love. We will experience travel at the speed of thought. Our lifespan will increase. There will be amazing breakthroughs in science and medicine. This new knowledge will lead us through the spiritual darkness of our present time into an enlightened new world. All of us, working together with a greater spiritual awareness, will finally create a beautiful, heavenly place here on Earth.

Our hopes and dreams for the new world are challenges that dare us to reach higher and try harder to complete our earthly mission. Everything we need to accomplish this is within ourselves. As we raise our vibrations, the invisible will become visible. The unknown will become known. We will be able to work side by side with our space brethren for the betterment of Earth. We will be able to see the nature spirits as they carry out their appointed tasks. We will be aware of the Angelic Beings as they bring us healing and protection. Our eyes, hearts, and minds will be opened, and we will experience a close, personal relationship with our Higher Self who has been our constant companion since the very beginning of our existence. We are standing on the edge of tomorrow looking into the future. Together we will triumphantly move into this new world, the Golden Age of Peace and Love.

Glossary

Alpha state: altered state of consciousness, slower heartbeat and respiration; state between waking and sleeping necessary for all psychic experiences.

Androgynous: both male and female.

Android: a highly advanced robot in the form of a human.

Angel: Latin *angelus,* meaning “messenger”; asexual; created Beings evolving on a different life path than humans.

Archangels: created Beings who are higher and more advanced than the rank of angel; also denotes all Angelic Beings above the grade of angel.

Ascended Master: person who has learned all lessons and cleared all karma, and does not need to return in a physical body.

Ashtar: Commander of the Intergalactic Fleet serving the Western Hemisphere.

Astral body: another name for emotional body; primary body used in fourth dimension; cord connects astral to physical body; astral several inches larger than the physical body and interpenetrates it.

Astral travel: also called astral projection or out-of-body, OOB; ability of astral body to leave physical body and function independently.

Astral world: also known as the fourth dimension, World Beyond; vibrates at a faster rate and interpenetrates the physical world.

Aura: portion of astral body that extends past the physical body; emotions and health affect colors.

Automatic writing: method of channeling information from the fourth dimension through writing; not recommended because it is a type of possession.

Brownie: nature spirit belonging to the Plant and Mineral Kingdom.

Channel: a person who is able to telepathically tune into the fourth dimension and relay the message either orally or in writing.

Clairaudience: the ability to hear sounds beyond normal range of hearing by using the sixth sense, ESP.

Clairvoyance: the ability to see or know things that are beyond normal vision by using the sixth sense, ESP.

Cosmic Lords: Archangels in charge of the universes.

Cosmic Truth: absolute truth.

Dark Forces: negative extraterrestrials, also known as fallen angels or Renegades.

Deeve: nature spirit of Persian folklore.

Dual consciousness: being consciously aware in the astral and physical bodies simultaneously.

Elf: nature spirit belonging to the Plant and Mineral Kingdom.

Emotional body: another name for the astral body; primary body used in the fourth dimension; several inches larger than physical body and interpenetrates it.

Energy body: inch larger, interpenetrates and energizes physical body; also called etheric body.

Extrasensory perception: referred to as ESP or the sixth sense; ability to see, feel, hear, and in rare cases, smell and taste in fourth dimension.

Extraterrestrials: beings not of Earth; Spiritual ETs, positive influence; Scientific ETs, neutral; Renegades, negative influence.

Fairy: smallest nature spirit belonging to the Air Kingdom; also used to refer to any nature spirit.

Fourth dimension: interpenetrates our third-dimensional, physical world; invisible to physical eyes because of higher vibrations.

Frankin: smallest nature spirit belonging to the Plant and Mineral Kingdom.

Gehenna: synonym for Hell.

Gnome: nature spirit belonging to the Plant and Mineral Kingdom.

Grays: humanoids who assist extraterrestrial space scientists.

Guardian Angel: also known as Twin Soul, Higher Self, Oversoul, Holy Spirit, God Self.

Higher Self: the part of a human that is perfect; the enigma is that human and Higher Self are one yet they express as two beings; also called Twin Soul, Guardian Angel.

Humanoid: extraterrestrial having a human form but robot by nature.

Inspirational writing: method of channeling information from the fourth dimension through writing.

Intergalactic Council: part of the Spiritual Hierarchy concerned with the betterment of the universe.

Intuition: spontaneously knowing something without conscious reasoning.

Leprechaun: nature spirit indigenous to Ireland.

Manikin: nature spirit indigenous to Germany.

Menehune: nature spirit indigenous to Hawaii.

Naiad: nature spirit belonging to the Water Kingdom; prefers fresh water.

Nature spirits: etheral beings who work in cooperation with nature in the fourth dimension.

Oceanid: smallest nature spirit belonging to the Water Kingdom.

Ouija board: method of contacting the fourth dimension; not recommended because of chance of deception.

Pendulum: method of contacting fourth dimension using a chain with a weight.

Peri: nature spirit of Persian folklore.

Photon Belt: huge mass of light and electromagnetic energy; as our solar system enters the Photon Belt, the whole solar system, including Earth, will be transformed.

Pineal gland: located near center of brain; considered the third eye and inner ear of astral body.

Planetary Lords: Archangels in charge of the various planets in the universe.

Renegades: negative extraterrestrials, part of the Dark Forces.

Sea nymph: nature spirit belonging to the Water Kingdom.

Silver cord: connects the physical and astral body at solar plexus.

Solar Lords: Archangels in charge of the various solar systems in the universe.

Soul body: extends past the astral body and interpenetrates the physical, energy, and astral body; the eternal, primary body above the fourth dimension.

Soul exchange: by arrangement of the Higher Selves, the

Soul of a person who is dying allows another Soul to take over the physical body; also referred to as a walk-in.

Soul mate: someone we have loved in many lives, as parent and child, as siblings, as lovers; may meet several soul mates in one lifetime, may meet none.

Spiritual path: leads back to perfection; the way of unconditional, nonjudgmental love.

Subconscious mind: records thoughts, words, and emotions and stores them as memories.

Superconscious mind: telepathic connection between people and their Higher Self.

Sylphs: nature spirits belonging to the Air Kingdom.

Tarot: method of receiving information from the fourth dimension by using special cards.

Telepathy: communication between one mind and another by using the sixth sense.

Trance state: very deep alpha state; also called hypnotic state.

Tree deva: largest nature spirit belonging to the Plant Kingdom.

Troll: nature spirit belonging to the Plant and Mineral Kingdom.

Twin Soul: the part of a person that is perfect; the enigma is that the human and Twin Soul are one yet express as two beings; does not incarnate in physical body; also called Higher Self, Guardian Angel.

Unconscious mind: the autonomic nervous system.

Visualize: to see or form a mental image in the mind.

White Light: God's healing, protecting energy coming

through the Higher Self.

World Beyond: another name for the fourth dimension, astral world, Heaven, Hell.

Zephyr: nature spirit belonging to the Air Kingdom.

Further Reading

Both ancient and modern seers have prophesied that between now and the year 2012 great earth changes will occur. Not only will we experience the effects of El Niño, La Niña , and the Photon Belt, but there is a possibility of other major disasters, including a polar shift.

In *Enlightenment: The Key to Survival in the 21st Century*, the companion volume to this book, FranCelia Woodward explains what enlightenment is and how it will help us survive in the new millennium. Enlightenment is a personal experience through which we are able to expand our consciousness beyond the limited physical plane and achieve cosmic consciousness. Every chapter is filled with valuable information that can change your life forever. When we become enlightened, we will understand that what is happening in our world is a part of a great cosmic plan, and even in the midst of chaos, we will be able to experience a deep sense of inner peace.

Both *Enlightenment: The Key to Survival in the 21st Century* and additional copies of *Exploring the World Beyond* are available at your local bookstore or may be ordered from:

About the Author

FranCelia Woodward received her degree in Psychology from Pepperdine University. She made the transition to parapsychology after the life-changing experience recounted in the Preface of this book. She retired after teaching for thirty years for the Los Angeles Board of Education, but she continues to teach classes in parapsychology. Mrs. Woodward has three sons and a daughter, as well as six grandchildren.

The author is clairvoyant and clairaudient and has touched many lives through her classes and counseling. She is the Northwest director of The Inner Voice, a non-profit organization dedicated to helping people discover their innate abilities.

Mrs. Woodward has written several books including *Enlightenment: The Key to Survival in the 21st Century,* the companion volume to *Exploring the World Beyond.* If you would like information about these books or would like to learn how to receive personal counseling, please send a stamped, self-addressed envelope to:

FranCelia Woodward
c/o The Inner Voice
84980 Chezem Road
Eugene, OR 97405